kids'
party
cakes

kids' party cakes

50 fun, fast and fabulous ideas

MURDOCH BOOKS

Contents

Introduction

There is nothing more exciting than creating a fabulous cake that your kids will love and remember for years to come. This book features creative and easy cakes that you can prepare with a minimum of fuss. They are adaptable for any occasion and many of the designs can be tailored to suit your child.

All the cakes in this book are suitable for beginners and step-by-step photographs will guide you along the way for the more challenging ones. Remember to always read through the recipe from start to finish before you begin—in fact, before you even start to prepare and shop for your ingredients. This is important whatever you are cooking but for cake decorating it is vital.

Make sure you set aside enough time to complete the cake without pressure. And if you are short of time, feel free to use a cake mix or purchase a plain cake and use the designs to make it your own.

The decorating time for each cake is indicated at the top of the recipe for easy reference. Any preparation and cooking times for the cake base is set out in The Basics chapter at the back of the book. Here you will also find helpful information about cake decorating ingredients and techniques that will guide you to cake success. A handy template sheet containing the basic outlines for the more unusual-shaped cakes can also be found at the back of the book.

This is a book of ideas as much as it is a book of cake designs. Allow your creative flair to change the colour or decorations on any of the cakes and make each one a special work of art—something that both you and your child will delight in.

Monsters & Animals

★ Mervin the Martian

22 cm (8½ inch) round
vanilla buttercake (recipe
page 142, see tip)

3 × 185 ml (6 fl oz/¾ cup)
large vanilla cupcakes
(see tip)

1½ quantities vanilla
buttercream (recipe
page 145)

Red food colouring

2 chocolate-coated mint
biscuits (cookies)

8 white chocolate melts

2 green candy-coated
chocolate buttons

7 milk bottle-shaped soft
white candies

6 banana-shaped soft
yellow candies

1 Use a sharp knife to level the tops of the cakes, if necessary. Tint the buttercream with the red food colouring to the desired colour.

2 For the eyes, position two of the large cupcakes at the top of the cake. For the feet, cut the remaining cupcake in half vertically and position at the bottom of the cake, as shown. Spread three-quarters of the red buttercream all over the cake.

3 For the eyes, position the biscuits on the large cupcakes. Using the picture as a guide, position the white chocolate melts on the biscuits using a little buttercream. For the pupils, secure the green candy-coated chocolate buttons on the white chocolate melts using a little buttercream.

4 For the teeth, stagger the milk bottle-shaped candies on the large cake, as shown. Using a piping (icing) bag fitted with a 1 cm (½ inch) round piping tip, pipe a squiggly line of red buttercream around the milk bottles to make a mouth. Using the picture as a guide, pipe small spikes around the top of each eye.

5 For the feet, position three banana-shaped candies on each foot to make toes and three white chocolate melts on the base of each foot to make suckers, as shown.

TIP: For this recipe you will need two quantities of vanilla buttercake. Spoon a ½ cup of the mixture into each of three greased 185 ml (6 fl oz/¾ cup) large (texas) cupcake/muffin tin holes and bake for 30 minutes. Spread the remaining cake mixture into a 22 cm (8½ inch) round cake tin and bake for 1 hour.

You will need a 30 cm (12 inch) square cake board for this cake.

Tint white sugar with yellow food colouring to make sand and use felt stars on the board.

★ Slithery Snake

Decorating Time: 1 hour

2 × 20 cm (8 inch) ring
  vanilla buttercakes
  (recipe page 142)
2 quantities vanilla
  buttercream (recipe
  page 145)
Purple, pink, blue and green
  food colourings
150 g (5½ oz) white
  fondant icing
Icing (confectioner's)
  sugar, sifted
2 yellow ring-shaped hard
  candies
2 brown mini candy-coated
  chocolate buttons
1 red jelly snake (gummy
  snake)

1   Cut both the ring cakes in half.
Cut one of the halves into two equal
pieces for the head and tail. Using
a small serrated knife, trim along the
top edges to give the cakes a rounded
shape. Place the three half-ring cakes
on the board to make a snake shape.
Place one smaller piece of cake on
each end of the snake for the head
and tail. Trim one end to a point for
the tail. Trim the other end to a wider
point for the head.

2   Tint the buttercream with the purple
food colouring to the desired colour.
Secure the cake pieces together with
a little buttercream. Reserve 1 tablespoon
for the dots. Spread the remaining purple
buttercream all over the snake.

3   Divide the fondant icing into three
pieces. Tint one piece with the pink food
colouring, one with the blue food colouring

and one with the green food colouring
to the desired colours. Knead each
colour on a work surface lightly dusted
with the sifted icing sugar until smooth.
Roll each piece of fondant on the work
surface to 4 mm (⅛ inch) thick. Using
2 cm (¾ inch), 3 cm (1¼ inch) and
4 cm (1½ inch) round cutters, cut out
spots from each colour.

4   Using the picture as a guide, stick
spots randomly on the snake. Using
a piping (icing) bag fitted with a 5 mm
(¼ inch) round tip, pipe purple dots over
the snake. Place the yellow candies and
brown buttons for the snake's eyes.

5   For the tongue, remove and discard
2 cm (¾ inch) from the tail of the red
jelly snake, then slice through the jelly
snake's head lengthways to make a
forked tongue. Position the jelly snake
onto the mouth.

★ Cuddly Bear

Decorating Time: 1 hour 15 minutes

2 × 20 cm (8 inch) round vanilla buttercakes (recipe page 142)

1 litre (35 fl oz/4 cup) vanilla buttercake, prepared in a pudding basin (recipe page 142)

2 quantities vanilla buttercream (recipe page 145)

Brown food colouring

5 × 5 cm (2 inch) bought jam rollettes (mini jelly cake rolls)

2 round chocolate-coated biscuits (cookies)

1 white marshmallow

3 brown candy-coated chocolate buttons

10 cm (4 inch) black licorice strap

1 red jellybean

50 cm (20 inch) × 2.5 cm (1 inch) wide red ribbon

1 Use a sharp knife to level the tops of the cakes, if necessary. Reserve ²⁄₃ cup of the buttercream. Tint the remaining buttercream with the brown food colouring to the desired colour.

2 For the body, sit one of the round cakes on the board and spread the top with a little brown buttercream. Sandwich the two round cakes together *(pic 1)*.

3 For the body, trim off a diagonal strip around the top and bottom edges of the cake sandwich to form rounded shapes, as shown. Sit the pudding-shaped cake on the body, as shown. Push two wooden skewers through the head and body to firmly secure them. Trim the skewers.

4 For the head, trim the pudding shape, as shown *(pic 2)*. To create arms and legs, cut a diagonal slice off one end of four of the rollettes and attach them to the body with skewers.

5 For the snout, cut a 1.5 cm (⅝ inch) slice off the remaining rollette and stick it onto the centre of the face with a skewer. For the ears, make two slits on the top of the head, then push one of the chocolate biscuits into each slit *(pic 3)*.

6 Thickly spread the brown buttercream over the whole cake. Rough up the buttercream with a palette knife so that it looks like fur. Spread the reserved uncoloured buttercream over the tummy, snout, ears and ends of the arms and legs. Rough up to make fur.

7 For the eyes, halve the marshmallows and stick a candy-coated chocolate button on each half using a dab of buttercream. Press the eyes in place.

8 Use thin strips of licorice for the lips, a triangular piece for the nose and a red jellybean for the mouth. Use the remaining candy-coated chocolate button for a belly button. Attach the ribbon bow with a dab of buttercream.

You will need a 30 cm (12 inch) round cake board for this cake.

Use a pizza cutter to cut thin licorice strips.

1 *Sandwich the two round cakes with a little buttercream.*

2 *Trim the body and head to form rounded shapes.*

3 *Make a slit for each ear and push the biscuits in place.*

★ Miss Priscilla

Decorating Time: 1 hour 20 minutes

22 cm (8½ inch) round vanilla buttercake (recipe page 142)

20 × 30 cm (8 × 12 inch) rectangular vanilla buttercake (recipe page 142)

2 quantities vanilla buttercream (recipe page 145)

Pink and green food colourings

Miss Priscilla template (see template sheet)

20 cm (8 inch) black licorice strap

2 white marshmallows

1 each of green, blue, red, orange and yellow mini candy-coated chocolate buttons

2 teaspoons coloured sprinkles

2 purple candy-coated chocolate buttons

2 pink mini marshmallows

You will need a 30 cm (12 inch) round cake board for this cake.

Use a pizza cutter to cut thin licorice strips.

1 Use a sharp knife to level the tops of the cakes, if necessary. Tint 1 cup of vanilla buttercream with the pink food colouring to the desired pale pink colour. Tint ½ cup of the remaining buttercream with the green food colouring to the desired colour. Tint the remaining buttercream with the pink food colouring to the desired dark pink colour. Reserve 1 tablespoon of the dark pink buttercream for the ears.

2 Position the large round cake, cut side down, towards the bottom of the cake board and secure with a little dark pink buttercream.

3 Place the template over the rectangular cake and secure with toothpicks. Cut out one round shape for the snout, two ear shapes and one triangle shape for the hat. Discard any leftover cake.

4 For the snout, using the picture as a guide, position the small cake round on top of the large round cake, securing with a little of the dark pink buttercream.

5 Using the picture as a guide, position the triangle hat and ears on top of the large round cake, securing with a little dark pink buttercream.

6 Spread the remaining dark pink buttercream all over the large cake. Spread the pale pink buttercream all over the snout and ears. Using the picture as a guide, spread the reserved dark pink buttercream in the centre of the ears. Spread the remaining green buttercream all over the hat.

7 Cut the licorice strap into thin strips and position the strips to outline all of the hat and to create a mouth and eyelashes. Using the picture as a guide, decorate the hat with the mini candy-coated chocolate buttons and sprinkles. For the eyes, attach candy-coated chocolate buttons to the marshmallows, securing with a little buttercream and place on the cake. Position mini marshmallows on the snout.

★ Flashy Fishy

Decorating Time: 1 hour 10 minutes

2 × 22 cm (8½ inch) round vanilla buttercakes (recipe page 142)

Flashy Fishy template (see template sheet)

2 quantities vanilla buttercream (recipe page 145)

Green and blue food colourings

Black and red writing gels

1 white marshmallow

12 yellow sugar-coated jubes (gummy candies), halved horizontally

10 green sugar-coated jubes (gummy candies), halved horizontally

10 purple sugar-coated jubes (gummy candies), halved horizontally

Candy-coated choc chips

1 Use a sharp knife to level the tops of the cakes, if necessary. Position the body template on one cake and secure with toothpicks. Cut out the mouth shape, using a small sharp knife. Place the other template pieces on the remaining cake, securing with toothpicks. Cut out around the pieces.

2 Using the picture as a guide, assemble the fish on the cake board, trimming the fins if they need it so that they will join the body neatly. Using the picture as a guide, divide the three striped sections on the body by lightly marking the cake with a sharp knife.

3 Reserve one-quarter of the buttercream. Divide the remaining buttercream into two bowls. Tint one bowl with the green food colouring to the desired colour. Tint the other bowl with the blue food colouring to the desired colour.

4 Spread the reserved uncoloured buttercream onto the face. Spread the blue buttercream over the middle back section and tail. Attach the fins to the cake as shown, using a little buttercream. Spread the first and third sections and the fins with the green buttercream.

5 Outline the sections and accent the tail using the black writing gel. Pipe around the edge of the mouth with the red writing gel.

6 For the eye, cut the marshmallow in half horizontally. Discard the remaining half marshmallow. Attach the eye. Using black writing gel, pipe a dot on the eye for the pupil. Arrange the jubes, cut side up, on the sections to create scales. To finish, sprinkle candy-coated choc chips on the tips of the tail.

★ Green Monster

Decorating Time: 1 hour 30 minutes

15 cm (6 inch) round vanilla
  buttercake (recipe page 142,
  see tip)
15 cm (6 inch) square vanilla
  buttercake (recipe page 142,
  see tip)
1 quantity vanilla buttercream
  (recipe page 145)
500 g (1 lb 2 oz) white
  fondant icing
Green, dark blue and
  black food colourings
Icing (confectioner's)
  sugar, sifted
Green Monster template
  (see template sheet)
Black writing gel

1   Use a sharp knife to level the tops of the cakes, if necessary. Cut the round cake in half (pic 1). Join the square cake and half round cake with a little buttercream, as shown (pic 2), and cover with buttercream. Reserve remaining half round cake for another use.

2   For the face, tint 380 g (13½ oz) of the fondant icing with the green food colouring to the desired colour. Knead on a work surface lightly dusted with the sifted icing sugar until smooth. Roll the fondant on the work surface to make a 35 cm (14 inch) square. Using a rolling pin, gently lift the fondant and place over the cake. Using warm dry hands, gently smooth the fondant down over the cake. Trim the edges (pic 3). Reserve all the trimmings.

3   For the hair, tint 60 g (2¼ oz) of the remaining fondant with the dark blue food colouring to the desired colour. Using the template, cut out the hair and attach to the head with a little

water. Texture the hair with lines using the rounded tip of a paintbrush handle.

4   For the face, make the eyebrows, lip and nose from the green fondant trimmings, using the picture as a guide. Using the template, make the ears from green fondant. For the eyes, colour the green fondant with extra green colouring and cut out the irises. For the mouth, tint 30 g (1 oz) of the remaining white fondant with the black food colouring. Using the template, cut out the mouth. Using the picture as a guide, make the teeth from the remaining white fondant. Using the template, make the eyes from the remaining white fondant. Using the picture as a guide, attach the facial features with a little water. Pipe an outline around the eyes and corners of the mouth with the black writing gel.

TIP: For this recipe you will need two quantities of vanilla buttercake. Spoon one quantity into each prepared tin and bake both for 30–35 minutes.

You will need a 30 cm (12 inch) round cake board for this cake.

1 *Level the tops of the cakes, if necessary.*

2 *Join the square cake and half round cake with a little buttercream.*

3 *Smooth the fondant over the cake and trim the edges.*

★ Mice and Cheese

Decorating Time: 1 hour

24 cm (9½ inch) round
  vanilla buttercake (recipe
  page 142, see tip)
2 × 80 ml (2½ fl oz/⅓ cup)
  vanilla cupcakes (see tip)
1 quantity vanilla buttercream
  (recipe page 145)
Grey and yellow food
  colourings
2 pink marshmallows, halved
4 brown mini candy-coated
  chocolate buttons
2 red mini candy-coated
  chocolate buttons
10 cm (4 inch) black licorice
  strap
500 g (1 lb 2 oz) white
  fondant icing
Icing (confectioner's)
  sugar, sifted

1   Use a sharp knife to level the tops of the cakes, if necessary. Tint ½ cup of the buttercream with the grey food colouring to the desired colour. Tint the remaining buttercream with the yellow food colouring to the desired colour. For the mice, spread the tops and sides of the cupcakes with grey buttercream.

2   For the ears, position the pink marshmallow halves on top of each large vanilla cupcake, using the picture as a guide. For the eyes and nose, position the brown and red candy-coated chocolate buttons, as shown.

3   For the whiskers, cut small strips of licorice to make 12 whiskers. Position six whiskers on each mouse. Cut 2 × 10 cm (4 inch) strips of licorice strap and position on each mouse to make a tail.

4   For the cheese, place the large cake, cut side down on the cake board. Using a melon baller or spoon, scoop out different sized holes over the top and side of the cake to represent Swiss

cheese. Spread a very thin layer of yellow buttercream over the cake and in the holes.

5   Tint the fondant icing using the yellow food colouring to the desired colour. Knead the fondant on a work surface lightly dusted with the sifted icing sugar until smooth. Roll the fondant on the work surface to about 4 mm (⅛ inch) thick, making a 35 cm (14 inch) circle. Using a rolling pin, gently lift the fondant and place over the cake. Using warm dry hands, gently smooth the fondant, moulding it into the cheese holes. Using the picture as a guide, position the mice on the cake and board.

TIP: For this recipe you will need two quantities of vanilla buttercake. Spoon ¼ cup of the mixture into each of two greased 80 ml (2½ fl oz/⅓ cup) cupcake/muffin tin holes and bake for 20 minutes. Spread the remaining cake mixture into a 24 cm (9½ inch) round cake tin and bake for 1 hour 10 minutes.

You will need a 40 cm
(16 inch) round cake
board for this cake.

Use a pizza cutter to cut
thin licorice strips.

★ Loopy Lion

Decorating Time: 1 hour

22 × 35 cm (8½ × 14 inch) rectangular vanilla butter-cake (recipe page 142)

1 quantity vanilla buttercream (recipe page 145)

Loopy Lion template (see template sheet)

2 tablespoons unsweetened cocoa powder, sifted

Yellow food colouring

2 brown candy-coated chocolate buttons

2 white marshmallows

20 cm (8 inch) black licorice strap

2 white chocolate melts

1 milk chocolate melt

1 red sugar-coated jube (gummy candy)

1 Use a sharp knife to level the top of the cake, if necessary. Place the cake on the cake board. Position the template on the cake and secure with toothpicks. Cut out around the lion's head shape using a small sharp knife. Beat the cocoa powder into one-third of the buttercream. Tint the remaining buttercream with the yellow food colouring to the desired colour.

2 For the face, spread the yellow buttercream in an oval shape on the centre of the cake.

3 For the mane, spread the chocolate buttercream over the remaining cake. Rough up the chocolate buttercream with a palette knife to resemble a mane.

4 For the eyes, stick one candy-coated chocolate button on each marshmallow with a dab of buttercream. Position the eyes in place. Use thin strips of licorice for the lips and whiskers.

5 For the ears, poke the white chocolate melts in place, using the picture as a guide. For the ear centres, cut one-third off the top of one of the milk chocolate melts and cut in half. Stick the ear centres on with a dab of buttercream.

6 For the nose, place the remaining part of the milk chocolate melt in place, as shown. For the mouth, trim the red jube into a tongue shape and place under the nose.

You will need a 25 x 35 cm (10 x 14 inch) rectangular cake board for this cake.

Use a pizza cutter to cut thin licorice strips.

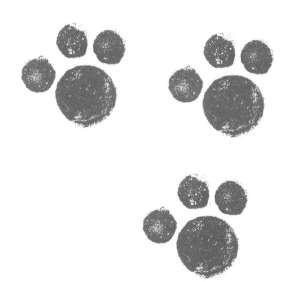

★ Bedtime Bunnies

Decorating Time: 1 hour 15 minutes

2 × 20 cm (8 inch) square
   vanilla buttercakes (recipe
   page 142)
1 quantity vanilla buttercream
   (recipe page 145)
Yellow and brown food
   colourings
6 large white marshmallows
320 g (11¼ oz) white
   fondant icing
3 orange mini candy-coated
   chocolate buttons
Black writing gel
Icing (confectioner's)
   sugar, sifted
10 coloured sugar flowers
   (see tip)
4 yellow mini candy-coated
   chocolate buttons
3 red mini candy-coated
   chocolate buttons

You will need a 30 cm (12 inch) square cake board for this cake.

1 Use a sharp knife to level the tops of the cakes, if necessary. Tint the buttercream with the yellow food colouring to the desired colour.

2 Using a serrated knife, cut one of the cakes in half vertically. Reserve one half of the cake for another use. Position the whole cake in the centre of the cake board and secure with a little buttercream. Using the picture as a guide, stand the remaining cake half, cut side down and rounded side facing out, on one end of the whole cake to form the bedhead. Secure with a little buttercream.

3 Spread the remaining buttercream all over the cakes. Position three of the marshmallows across the bed to create pillows. Halve the remaining marshmallows and position two halves, alongside each other, below each pillow to create the three bunnies' bodies underneath the blanket.

4 Tint 120 g (4¼ oz) of the fondant icing with the brown food colouring to the desired colour. Reserve 40 g (1½ oz) for the ears and paws. Roll the remaining brown fondant into three round shapes to create the bunnies' heads. Divide the reserved fondant into three portions and mould two ears and two paws from each portion of the fondant. Attach the ears to the heads with a little water.

5 Position the heads on the pillows and secure with a little water. Position orange mini candy-coated chocolate buttons on the bunnies' faces for the noses and secure with a little water. Pipe eyes and ear centres with the black writing gel.

6 For the bedspread, knead the remaining white fondant on a work surface lightly dusted with the sifted icing sugar until smooth. Roll the fondant out on the work surface to a 25 cm (10 inch) square and trim the edges. Using the back of a small knife, lightly score the bedspread in a patchwork pattern.

7 Using a rolling pin, lift the fondant over the bottom of the cake, folding the top of the fondant over until just under the bunnies' heads. Trim the draped fondant on the board to neaten the shape of the bedspread.

8 Position the bunnies' paws on the bedspread and secure with a little water. Position the sugar flowers on the bedspread, securing with a little water. Position the yellow and red mini candy-coated chocolate buttons around the bedhead.

TIP: Sugar flowers are small flowers made from fondant icing. They are available in the cake decorating section of most supermarkets.

★ Saltwater Sam

Decorating Time: 1 hour 30 minutes

2.5 litre (10 cup) vanilla buttercake, prepared in a dolly varden cake tin (recipe page 142, see tip)

48 × 20 ml (½ fl oz) vanilla mini cupcakes in silver foil cases (see tip)

3 quantities vanilla buttercream (recipe page 145)

Orange and blue food colourings

2 tablespoons sugar

1 red sour strap or fruit strap

2 blue candy-coated chocolate buttons

2 white marshmallows

1 red jelly snake (gummy snake)

70 fruit-flavoured cereal rings

1 sheet blue cellophane

1   Use a sharp knife to level the tops of the cakes, if necessary. Tint the buttercream with the orange food colouring to the desired colour. Place the sugar into a snaplock bag. Add a few drops of the blue food colouring. Seal the bag and rub the sugar through the bag until the sugar is tinted blue.

2   Position the dolly varden cake in the centre of the board, as shown, and secure with a little orange buttercream.

3   Spread the remaining orange buttercream all over the large cake and over the base and sides of the mini cupcakes, leaving the tops un-iced. Using the picture as a guide, position the mini cupcakes upside down on the board to form octopus tentacles.

4   For the hair, use kitchen scissors to cut the sour strap in half. Then cut 5 mm (¼ inch) wide strips through each half, leaving a 2 cm (¾ inch) solid piece at one end. Press the sour strap halves into the top of the large cake, as shown.

5   For the eyes, attach one blue candy-coated chocolate button on each marshmallow, securing with a little buttercream. Position the marshmallows on the face, as shown. Cut 1.5 cm (⅝ inch) off each end of the jelly snake and position the remainder for the mouth. Using the picture as a guide, decorate the mini cupcakes with the fruit-flavoured cereal rings.

6   Sprinkle the blue-coloured sugar over the board. Cut the cellophane into thin strips and position on the board to make waves, as shown.

TIP: For this recipe you will need three quantities of vanilla buttercake. Spoon 3 level teaspoons of the mixture into each of 48 greased 20 ml (½ fl oz) mini cupcake/muffin tin holes and bake for 10 minutes. Spread the remaining cake mixture into a 2.5 litre (10 cup) dolly varden cake tin and bake for 1 hour 15 minutes.

You will need a 60 cm (24 inch) round cake board for this cake.

★ March of the Lady Beetles

Decorating Time: 1 hour

12 × 80 ml (2½ fl oz/⅓ cup)
vanilla cupcakes in red
paper cases (recipe
page 142)
1 quantity vanilla
buttercream (recipe
page 145)
Red and black food
colourings
1 m (40 inch) black
licorice strap
70 g (2½ oz) white
fondant icing
Black writing gel

1   Use a sharp knife to level the tops of the cupcakes, if necessary. Tint the buttercream with the red food colouring to the desired colour. Using a palette knife or spatula, spread the buttercream over the tops of the cupcakes.

2   Using a pizza cutter, trim the licorice strap into shoestring-like lengths. Using the licorice strips, mark out half circles on the cupcakes to resemble the outlines of the lady beetles' faces, as shown. Use the remaining licorice to place down the middle of the remaining parts of the cupcakes to separate the wings.

3   Tint 50 g (1¾ oz) of the fondant icing with the black food colouring. Roll pea-sized pieces of the black fondant into small balls. You will need six for each cupcake. Position three balls on each wing of each lady beetle.

4   For the eyes, roll the remaining white fondant into pea-sized balls. For the pupils, pipe a small dot on each eye using the black writing gel. Position the eyes on the cupcakes, as shown.

You will need a 40 cm (16 inch) square cake board for this cake.

Use icing flowers and spearmint leaf-shaped sugar-coated jubes to decorate the board.

★ Clarissa Cat

Decorating Time: 1 hour 15 minutes

24 cm (9½ inch) round
  vanilla buttercake (recipe
  page 142)
1 quantity vanilla buttercream
  (recipe page 145)
Orange, black, ivory, pink
  and red food colourings
100 g (3½ oz) white
  fondant icing
Icing (confectioner's)
  sugar, sifted
Clarissa Cat template
  (see template sheet)
30 cm (12 inch) × 5 mm
  (¼ inch) wide pink ribbon
30 cm (12 inch) × 5 mm
  (¼ inch) wide orange ribbon
10 cm (4 inch) black
  licorice strap

1   Use a sharp knife to level the top of the cake, if necessary. Trim the cake to a slight oval shape and place on the board.

2   Tint one-quarter of the vanilla buttercream with the orange food colouring to the desired colour. Spread the remaining uncoloured buttercream over the entire cake. Spread the orange buttercream on the cake in patches. Using a fork, rough up the buttercream to resemble cat fur.

3   Divide the fondant icing in half. Tint half with the black food colouring and the other half with the ivory food colouring to match the uncoloured buttercream. Knead both fondants on a work surface lightly dusted with the sifted icing sugar until smooth.

4   For the ears, roll the ivory fondant on the work surface to 4 mm (⅛ inch) thick. Position the larger ear template on the ivory fondant and cut out the two ears.

5   For the inner ears, tint the remaining ivory fondant with the pink food colouring to the desired colour. Knead the pink fondant on a work surface lightly dusted with the sifted icing sugar until smooth. Roll the pink fondant on the work surface to 4 mm (⅛ inch) thick. Position the smaller ear template on the fondant and cut out two inner ears. Stick the pink inner ears onto the ivory larger ears with a little water. Position the ears on the cake.

6   Tie a bow with the two ribbons, as shown, and place near the ear.

7   For the eyes and nose, mould the black fondant to make the eyes and nose and position on the face, using the picture as a guide. Tint a small amount of the remaining pink fondant with the red food colouring to the desired colour. Roll into a thin sausage for the mouth and position on the cake.

8   For the whiskers, cut the licorice strap lengthways into thin strips using a pizza cutter or sharp knife and position on the cake, using the picture as a guide.

You will need a 30 cm (12 inch) round cake board for this cake.

★ Daniel the Dinosaur

Decorating Time: 1 hour 20 minutes

20 × 30 cm (8 × 12 inch) rectangular vanilla buttercake (recipe page 142)

2 quantities vanilla buttercream (recipe page 145)

Purple food colouring

Daniel the Dinosaur template (see template sheet)

Black writing gel

2 white mini marshmallows

12 yellow candy-coated chocolate buttons

12 green mini candy-coated chocolate buttons

1   Use a sharp knife to level the top of the cake, if necessary. Tint the vanilla buttercream with the purple food colouring to the desired colour.

2   Position the template on the cake, as shown, and secure with toothpicks. Cut out around the dinosaur body using a small sharp knife *(pic 1)*. Using the remainder of the cake, position the template and cut out the tail and head *(pic 2)*.

3   Secure the head and tail pieces to the body of the dinosaur using a little buttercream. Press into place against the body *(pic 3)*.

4   Spread the remaining purple buttercream over the whole dinosaur cake, including the sides. With the template as a guide, use a skewer or toothpick to draw the outlines and all the features onto the dinosaur. Using the black writing gel, pipe the outline and features of the dinosaur over the lines drawn.

5   For the eyes, flatten the two white marshmallows slightly and place them into position. For the pupils, pipe a small black dot on each marshmallow using the black writing gel. Arrange the candy-coated chocolate buttons randomly over the cake.

You will need a 30 cm (12 inch) round cake board for this cake.

Use candy-coated buttons for the sun.

1 *Cut out around the dinosaur body.*

2 *Cut the head and tail using the remainder of the cake.*

3 *Secure the pieces of the dinosaur using a little buttercream.*

★ Jetstream Jumbo

Decorating Time: 1 hour 30 minutes

9 × 19 cm (3½ × 7½ inch) loaf vanilla buttercake (recipe page 142)

20 × 30 cm (8 × 12 inch) rectangular vanilla buttercake (recipe page 142)

1½ quantities vanilla buttercream (recipe page 145)

Green and blue food colourings

Jetstream Jumbo template (see template sheet)

60 cm (24 inch) black licorice strap

20 white rectangular mini hard candies

12 each of yellow and orange mini candy-coated chocolate buttons

15 red mini candy-coated chocolate buttons

1   Use a sharp knife to level the tops of the cakes, if necessary. Tint ⅔ cup of the buttercream using the green food colouring to the desired colour. Tint the remaining buttercream using the blue food colouring to the desired colour.

2   For the plane body, use a small sharp knife to trim one end of the loaf cake into a slightly pointed shape, removing the two corners *(pic 1)*. Position the cake in the centre of the cake board and secure with a little green buttercream.

3   For the wings and tail, position the template on the rectangular cake and secure with toothpicks. Cut out around the two wing shapes and three tail pieces using a small sharp knife *(pic 1)*.

4   Spread the green buttercream all over the body of the plane *(pic 2)*. Spread the blue buttercream all over the wings and tail. Using the picture

as a guide, position the wings on either side of the plane body and secure with a little buttercream. Position the tail on the back and top of the plane's body and secure with wooden skewers (remove before serving).

5   For the jet engines, cut two 25 cm (10 inch) lengths from the licorice strap. Roll up the two lengths for the jet engines and reserve.

6   Using the picture as a guide, decorate the cake with the white rectangular mini hard candies to create the windows and use mini candy-coated chocolate buttons on the wings and tail.

7   For the jet engines, position the reserved rolled licorice straps on the front of the wings. Cut some of the remaining licorice strap into thin strips and position them to outline the front windows of the jet.

You will need a 40 cm (16 inch) square cake board for this cake.

Use a pizza cutter to cut thin licorice strips.

Use sprinkles and mini jubes (gumdrops) on the board.

1   Cut all the shapes using the template and a sharp knife.

2   Cover the jet body with green buttercream.

★ Choo-Choo Train

Decorating Time: 1 hour 30 minutes

56 coloured ice-block (popsicle) sticks

Two 9 × 19 cm (3½ × 7½ inch) loaf vanilla buttercakes (recipe page 142)

2 × 5 cm (2 inch) bought jam rollettes (mini jelly cake rolls)

2 quantities vanilla buttercream (recipe page 145)

Red, blue, yellow and green food colourings

1 m (40 inch) black licorice strap

1 large white marshmallow

18 sprinkle-coated chocolate buttons

2 ice-cream wafers

2 orange candy-coated chocolate buttons

10 musk- or fruit-flavoured candy sticks

10 round coloured candies

20 coloured jellybeans

3 × 2.5 cm (1 inch) lengths licorice twists

1 For the track, using the picture as a guide, arrange the ice-block sticks along the cake board.

2 Use a sharp knife to level the tops of the cakes, if necessary. Cut one-third off one cake and cut the other cake into three even pieces. To make the engine, sit one of the small pieces of cake on top of the large piece and position on the train track. Use the rollettes, positioned at right angles, to make the train funnel.

You will need a 60 cm (24 inch) square cake board for this cake.

3 Divide the buttercream in half and tint one portion with the red food colouring to the desired colour. Divide the remaining buttercream into three bowls. Tint one portion blue, one portion yellow and one portion green. Spread the red buttercream over the engine and base of the funnel. Spread the blue buttercream over the top of the funnel. Spread each of the carriages with a different coloured buttercream.

4 Line up the carriages on the track behind the engine. Cut the licorice strap into thin strips and, using the picture as a guide, outline the engine and carriages with licorice strips. Position the marshmallow on the engine's funnel to resemble smoke.

5 For the wheels, position two sprinkle-coated chocolate buttons along the bottom of each side of the carriages and three along

each side of the engine. For the carriage windows, place an ice-cream wafer on each side of the cabin.

6 For the lights, press the two orange candy-coated buttons into the front of the engine. Pile the candy sticks on one carriage, round coloured candies on another and jellybeans on the third carriage. Connect each of the carriages with a piece of licorice twist.

45

Bang, Whir, Whack

★ Tailside

Decorating Time: 1 hour

26 × 35 cm (10½ × 14 inch)
  rectangular vanilla
  buttercake (recipe
  page 142)
Tailside template
  (see template sheet)
1½ quantities vanilla
  buttercream (recipe
  page 145)
**Purple and green food
  colourings**
**Four 8 cm (3¼ inch) bought
  cream-filled chocolate
  cake rollettes**
**4 striped sour straps
  or fruit straps**
**22 blue candy-coated
  chocolate buttons**
**20 purple candy-coated
  chocolate buttons**

1 Use a sharp knife to level the top of the cake, if necessary, then turn over. Position the template on the cake and secure with toothpicks. Cut out the skateboard shape using a small sharp knife *(pic 1)*.

2 For the tail, cut down into the blunt end of the skateboard at a 45 degree angle, as shown. Reserve the piece for the rear wedge *(pic 2)*.

3 Tint ¾ cup of the buttercream with the purple food colouring to the desired colour. Tint the remaining buttercream with the green food colouring to the desired colour.

4 For the wheels, cover each of the chocolate cake rollettes with purple buttercream. Place two chocolate cake rolls, end to end, about 1 cm (½ inch)

apart on the cake board. Sit the other pair parallel, 11 cm (4¼ inches) away, as shown. Position a piece of leftover cake, the same height as the rollettes, in the gap between them as support for the cake.

5 Spread the green buttercream all over the top, sides and wedge of the cake. Carefully lift the skateboard onto the wheels.

6 For the stripes, create two 30 cm (12 inch) lengths from the sour straps. Trim one end of each strap on a slight angle to fit the nose of the skateboard. Position the two strips parallel down the board. Position one row of candy-coated chocolate buttons, alternating the colours, beside each sour strap. Position a blue candy-coated chocolate button on the end of each wheel.

You will need a 35 x 25 cm (14 x 10 inch) rectangular cake board for this cake.

1 *Using the template, cut out the shape of the skateboard.*

2 *Trim the back of the board and use the trim for the rear wedge.*

★ Big Red Bus

Decorating Time: 1 hour 30 minutes

26 × 35 cm (10½ × 14 inch) rectangular chocolate mud cake (recipe page 144)

2 quantities vanilla buttercream (recipe page 145)

Red food colouring

4 chocolate-coated mint biscuits (cookies)

4 white chocolate melts

1 m (40 inch) black licorice strap

150 g (5½ oz) white fondant icing

Icing (confectioner's) sugar, sifted

Black writing gel

4 orange candy-coated chocolate buttons

2 chocolate-coated licorice bullets

1 Use a sharp knife to level the top of the cake, if necessary. Cut the cake into three 10 × 20 cm (4 × 8 inch) pieces.

2 Tint the buttercream with the red food colouring to the desired colour. Stack the three cake pieces on top of one another, securing with a little red buttercream between layers. Position the cake on the board, securing with a little red buttercream. Spread the red buttercream over the top and sides of the cake.

3 For the wheels, position the four chocolate-coated mint biscuits on the sides of the cake. Using a little butter-cream, attach the white chocolate melts to make hubcaps. Position four 1 × 8 cm (½ × 3¼ inch) licorice strips around the top of the biscuits to make wheel arches and secure with a little buttercream. Using the picture as a guide, position a very thin 50 cm (20 inch) licorice strip around the sides and front of the cake to separate the two levels of the bus.

4 For the windows, roll the white fondant on a work surface lightly dusted with the sifted icing sugar to about 4 mm (⅛ inch) thick. Using rectangular cutters or a sharp knife,

cut 16 rectangles each 2 × 4 cm (¾ × 1½ inch). Using the picture as a guide, position eight windows in two rows on each side of the bus. Cut one 2 × 8 cm (¾ × 3¼ inch) rectangle from fondant and position on the lower back of the bus. Cut two 6 × 8 cm (2½ × 3¼ inch) rectangles from fondant. Position one on the top half of the back of the bus. Cut a third from the remaining rectangle to make two front windows and position on the front of the bus, as shown.

5 For the registration plates, cut two 1 × 2 cm (½ × ¾ inch) rectangles from the white fondant. Using the black writing gel, write numbers and letters on the registration plates.

6 For the bumper bars, cut two 2 × 12 cm (¾ × 4½ inch) licorice strips and position on the front and back of the cake. Using a little buttercream, position the orange candy-coated chocolate buttons to make headlights and rear tail lights. For side mirrors, position the chocolate bullets on each side of the cake. Position the registration plates on the front and back of bus, securing with a little buttercream.

You will need a 24 cm (9½ inch) square cake board for this cake.

Use chocolate-coated licorice bullets to make a road on the board.

★ Match Point

Decorating Time: 1 hour 15 minutes

25 cm (10 inch) square
  vanilla buttercake
  (recipe page 142)
2 quantities vanilla
  buttercream (recipe
  page 145)
Blue and black food
  colourings
4 striped sour straps
  or fruit straps
250 g (9 oz) white
  fondant icing
Icing (confectioner's)
  sugar, sifted
1 m (40 inch) black
  licorice strap

1 Use a sharp knife to level the
top of the cake, if necessary. Split
the cake into two layers and place
each layer side by side. Using the
picture as a guide, cut the oval part
of the racquet from one of the squares
and the handle from the other. Using
a small sharp knife trim off the edges
along the top of the handle to give
a rounded finish.

2 Tint three-quarters of the buttercream
with the blue food colouring to the desired
colour. Spread the blue buttercream all
over the oval section of the tennis racquet.
Tint the remaining buttercream with the
black food colouring. Spread the black
buttercream all over the handle. Cut the
sour straps in half and lay over the handle,
as shown.

3 For the face of the racquet, knead
the white fondant icing on a work
surface lightly dusted with the sifted
icing sugar until smooth. Roll the
fondant on the work surface to
about 4 mm (1/8 inch) thick. Cut out
an oval shape about 2.5 cm (1 inch)
smaller in diameter than the oval
of the tennis racquet. Position the
fondant oval on the middle of the
racquet head to create the face
of the racquet.

4 For the racquet strings, use
a pizza cutter to slice the licorice
strap lengthways into 2 mm (1/16 inch)
thick strips. Using a fine paintbrush
and water, mark a grid pattern on
the fondant to mark out the racquet
strings. Position the licorice strips over
the marked outlines for the strings.
Position strips of licorice around the
edge of the racquet head to highlight
the face of the racquet.

You will need a 25 x 50 cm
(10 x 20 inch) rectangular
cake board
for this cake.

★ Vroom Vroom Racing Car

Decorating Time: 1 hour 20 minutes

20 × 30 cm (8 × 12 inch) rectangular vanilla buttercake (recipe page 142)

9 × 19 cm (3½ × 7½ inch) loaf vanilla buttercake (recipe page 142)

Vroom Vroom Racing Car template (see template sheet)

1½ quantities vanilla buttercream (recipe page 145)

Yellow and red food colourings

2 × 1 m (40 inch) black licorice straps

8 round chocolate biscuits (cookies)

4 peppermints

2 black licorice twists

2 yellow mini jubes (gumdrops)

1 white marshmallow

3 licorice allsorts, halved

2 yellow round sugar-coated jubes (gummy candies)

10 cm (4 inch) square black cardboard

You will need a 25 x 30 cm (10 x 12 inch) rectangular cake board for this cake.

1 Use a sharp knife to level the tops of the cakes, if necessary. Position the chassis template onto the rectangular cake and secure with toothpicks. Cut out the chassis shape using a small sharp knife (pic 1). Shape the loaf cake by shaving a slice off either side of the cake so that the sides taper in. Then, starting from almost halfway along, shave the front at a 45 degree angle (pic 2).

2 Tint ⅓ cup of the buttercream with the yellow food colouring to the desired colour. Tint the remaining buttercream with the red food colouring to the desired colour. Position the chassis on the cake board and cover with the red buttercream (pic 3). Lift the cabin onto the chassis then cover with the red buttercream.

3 Using a piping (icing) bag fitted with a 5 mm (¼ inch) tip, pipe narrow stripes of the yellow buttercream down the centre and sides of the car, as shown. Cut the licorice into long thin strips. Position the licorice strips, as shown.

4 For each wheel and tyre, sandwich two of the chocolate-coated biscuits together with a little buttercream and wrap 18 cm (7 inch) of licorice strap around the outside, securing with a little buttercream. Repeat with the remaining biscuits to make four wheels. Attach a mint to the centre of each wheel with a little buttercream and position the wheels.

5 For the rear spoiler, push a toothpick through a 4 cm (1½ inch) licorice twist, then through one end of a 10 cm (4 inch) licorice strap and into a mini jube, as shown. Repeat on the other end of the strap and stick onto the car. For the helmet, attach a small square of licorice to the marshmallow.

6 Decorate the car with licorice allsorts. Use the yellow jubes for headlights. Cut out the child's birthday age from the cardboard and position on the bonnet.

1 *Position the template and cut out the chassis using a small sharp knife.*

2 *Shape the loaf cake to form the cabin of the racing car.*

3 *Cover the chassis with red buttercream.*

★ Electric Guitar

Decorating Time: 1 hour 30 minutes

Two 20 × 30 cm (8 × 12 inch) rectangular vanilla buttercakes (recipe page 142)

Electric Guitar template (see template sheet)

2½ quantities vanilla buttercream (recipe page 145)

1 tablespoon unsweetened cocoa powder, sifted

Blue food colouring

2 × 1 m (40 inch) black licorice straps

50 g (1¾ oz) triangular chocolate and nougat bar

6 brown candy-coated chocolate buttons

4 chocolate-coated licorice bullets

7 red candy-coated chocolate buttons

1 marshmallow, halved

1   Use a sharp knife to level the tops of the cakes, if necessary. Cut one of the cakes into thirds lengthways and leave the other whole. Position the cakes on the cake board, as shown, joining with a little buttercream (pic 1). Position the template on the cakes and secure with toothpicks. Mark the centre area, which will be covered with uncoloured buttercream, onto the cake by piercing through the paper with a skewer. Cut out around the guitar shape using a small sharp knife (pic 2). Trim the guitar's neck if it is too wide. Using one of the offcuts, add some extra length to the guitar's neck, as shown, joining with a little buttercream. Trim the end into a curve.

2   Reserve ½ cup of the buttercream. Mix another ½ cup of the buttercream with the cocoa. Tint the remaining buttercream with the blue food colouring to the desired colour. Cover the middle part of the guitar with the uncoloured buttercream, using your skewer marks as a guide. Cover a 10 cm (4 inch) tip at the end of the neck and the rest of the guitar's body with the blue buttercream. Cover the rest of the neck with the brown buttercream. Cut the licorice into thin strips to outline the white part of the guitar.

3   Using the picture as a guide, position six triangles of chocolate and the brown candy-coated chocolate buttons for the tuning pegs. Cut out two 1 × 7 cm (½ × 2¾ inch) long strips of licorice. Lay them across the middle of the cake and add a chocolate bullet on either end of them. Cut the licorice strap into six thin strips about 55 cm (22 inch) long and run them along the length of the guitar for the strings. Position a strip of licorice over the end of the strings at the neck end. Using the picture as a guide, decorate the guitar with the red candy-coated chocolate buttons and marshmallow halves.

You will need a 30 × 80 cm (12 × 31½ inch) rectangular cake board for this cake.

Use a pizza cutter to cut thin licorice strips.

Use a striped ribbon for the guitar strap.

1 *Cut and position the cakes on the board before cutting the shape.*

2 *Cut out the guitar shape and mark centre area using skewers.*

★ Little Blue Sail Boat —

Decorating Time: 1 hour 10 minutes + freezing time

4 litres (1 gallon) vanilla
   ice cream, softened

400 g (14 oz) white
   fondant icing

Red, blue and yellow
   food colourings

Icing (confectioner's)
   sugar, sifted

Little Blue Sail Boat template
   (see template sheet)

1 quantity vanilla
   buttercream (recipe
   page 145)

4 black licorice tubes

9 large silver cachous
   (edible silver balls)

5 red ring-shaped hard
   candies

1 Line the base and side of a 25 cm (10 inch) round springform cake tin with plastic wrap. Spoon the softened ice cream into the prepared tin and smooth the top with a spatula. Cover and freeze overnight.

2 Tint 100 g (3½ oz) of the fondant icing using the red food colouring to the desired colour. Leave the remaining fondant uncoloured.

3 For the sails, knead the white fondant on a work surface lightly dusted with the sifted icing sugar until smooth. Roll the white fondant on the work surface to 5 mm (¼ inch) thick. Position the sail templates on the white fondant. Using a sharp knife, cut out the two sails. Reserve the trimmings.

4 For the sail stripes, knead the red fondant on a work surface lightly dusted with the sifted icing sugar until smooth. Roll out the red fondant on the work surface to 5 mm (¼ inch) thick. Using a ruler and pizza cutter or sharp knife, cut 1 cm (½ inch) wide strips of red fondant. Using a paintbrush and a little water, stick the red strips 1 cm (½ inch) apart onto the white sails and trim to fit. Set aside to dry.

5 For the boat, take the ice-cream cake from the freezer and remove from the cake tin, retaining the circle shape. Using a large sharp knife cut the ice-cream cake in half. Place half on a tray and return to the freezer. Return the remaining ice cream to the freezer and reserve for another use.

6 Tint three-quarters of the buttercream using the blue food colouring to the desired dark blue colour. Remove the ice-cream cake from the freezer and spread the blue buttercream all over. Return to the freezer. Tint the remaining buttercream pale blue and reserve until ready to serve.

7 Tint some trimmings of the white fondant using the yellow food colouring to the desired colour. Knead the yellow fondant on a work surface lightly dusted with the sifted icing sugar until smooth. Roll the yellow fondant on the work surface to 3 mm (⅛ inch) thick. Using the flag template, cut out the flag from the yellow fondant. Cover with plastic wrap and set aside until ready to serve.

8 Just before serving and using the picture as a guide, secure licorice tubes onto the cake board with a little buttercream to make the mast of the boat. Using a little water and a paintbrush, stick the fondant sails onto the board on both sides of the mast. Then stick the small flag above the mast. Spread the pale blue buttercream on the board under the mast. Using a spatula, create swirl marks to create the waves, as shown.

9 Remove the boat from the freezer and place on the waves. Decorate the boat with the cachous and position the candy rings as portholes. Serve immediately.

You will need a 30 cm (12 inch) square cake board for this cake.

Cut licorice into seagull shapes for the board.

─── ★ Dumpy the Tip Truck

Decorating Time: 1 hour 20 minutes

Two 9 × 19 cm (3½ × 7½ inch) loaf vanilla buttercakes (recipe page 142)

1½ quantities vanilla buttercream (recipe page 145)

Green food colouring

2 × 60 g (2¼ oz) chocolate-coated caramel bars

1.5 m (60 inch) black licorice strap

6 chocolate-coated mint biscuits (cookies)

125 g (4½ oz) chocolate-coated sultanas (golden raisins)

1 ice-cream wafer

2 orange round sugar-coated jubes (gummy candies)

1 chocolate-coated licorice bullet

24 candy-coated chocolate buttons

125 g (4½ oz) chocolate-coated malt balls, halved

1   Use a sharp knife to level the tops of the cakes, if necessary. Reserve one-third of the buttercream. Tint the remaining buttercream with the green food colouring to the desired colour.

2   Cut the lid off an egg carton and trim the edges so that it will sit flat. Wrap the lid in paper and sit it on the cake board, cut side down to elevate the cake. Cut one of the cakes in half horizontally. For the tray, use a spoon to scoop out a shallow hollow from one of the cake halves, leaving a 1.5 cm (⅝ inch) border (pic 1).

3   Cut one-third off the other loaf cake. Stand the short piece on its cut side on the front of the egg carton. Stand the longer piece behind so that they look like the bonnet (hood) and cabin of the truck. Sit the whole cake half behind the cabin on the back of the egg carton to form the base of the tray. Join the pieces together with uncoloured buttercream (pic 2).

4   Spread the green buttercream over the truck, leaving the tray and spaces for the windscreen and windows (pic 3).

5   Cut the chocolate bars in half diagonally through the long side and place on the base of the truck to support the tray. Position the tray and cover with two-thirds of the remaining uncoloured buttercream. Spread the remaining uncoloured buttercream over the window and windscreen spaces.

6   Outline the windows and bonnet with thin strips of licorice and fix handles on the doors. Place a strip of licorice along each side of the truck. For the wheels, position the biscuits and secure a sultana to each wheel using a little buttercream. For the grill, trim the ice-cream wafer to fit and place it on the front of the truck. Position the orange jubes for the head-lights, a chocolate bullet for the aerial and the candy-coated chocolate buttons on the sides and back. Fill the tray with the malt balls and remaining sultanas.

You will need a 15 x 30 cm (6 x 12 inch) rectangular cake board for this cake.

Decorate the board with chocolate bullets.

1   *Scoop out a hollow to form the tray of the truck.*

2   *Cut the cake shapes to form the cabin and bonnet of the tip truck.*

3   *Cover the body, cabin and bonnet with green buttercream.*

Decorating Time: 1 hour 15 minutes

2 × 2.5 litre (10 cup) vanilla buttercakes, each prepared in a dolly varden tin (recipe page 142)

1 quantity vanilla buttercream (recipe page 145)

1.5 kg (3 lb 5 oz) white fondant icing

Black and red food colourings

Icing (confectioner's) sugar, sifted

1 Use a sharp knife to level the tops of the cakes, if necessary. Sandwich the two buttercakes together at the cake bases with a little of the buttercream to make a football shape. Secure with a long wooden skewer, pushed through one end of the football to the other (remove the skewer before serving). Trim a slice off the base of the football so that it sits flat on the board. Make the ends of the football slightly pointy by joining on little pieces of extra cake (from the trimmings) securing with some of the buttercream.

2 Spread a thin layer of buttercream over the football. Reserve 40 g (1½ oz) of the fondant icing for the laces. Tint 80 g (2¾ oz) of the remaining fondant with the black food colouring. Knead the fondant on a work surface dusted lightly with the sifted icing sugar until smooth. Tint the remaining fondant with the red food colouring to the desired colour. Knead on the work surface until smooth.

3 Roll the red fondant on the work surface to about 3 mm (⅛ inch) thick and large enough to cover the cake. Using a rolling pin, gently lift the fondant onto the cake. Using warm dry hands smooth the fondant over the cake, gently easing it under the cake, trying not to form pleats. Trim off any excess fondant and smooth with your hands.

4 For the name, roll the black fondant on the work surface to about 5 mm (¼ inch) thick. Cut out the letters using cutters or a sharp knife, and attach to the cake using a little water. For the laces, roll white fondant into a thin sausage, flatten slightly and cut into five 3 cm (1¼ inch) lengths. Using the end of a paintbrush, make 10 small holes in the top of the cake for the laces to fit into. Moisten the holes lightly with a little water and insert the ends of the laces into each hole. Using a fork, mark the football to create the stitching.

You will need a 15 cm (6 inch) round cake board for this cake.

Use small chocolate mint sticks to prop up the football and green felt for grass on the board.

★ The Big Bash

Decorating Time: 1 hour 20 minutes

20 × 30 cm (8 × 12 inch)
rectangular vanilla
buttercake (recipe
page 142, see tip)
1 × 185 ml (6 fl oz/¾ cup)
large vanilla cupcake
(see tip)
1½ quantities vanilla
buttercream (recipe
page 145)
Red and brown food
colourings
⅓ cup chocolate sprinkles
White writing gel

1   Use a sharp knife to level the tops of the cakes, if necessary. Tint ¼ cup of the buttercream with the red food colouring to the desired colour. Tint the remaining buttercream with the brown food colouring to the desired colour.

2   For the ball, trim the cupcake into a ball shape and spread with half the red buttercream, wrap firmly in plastic wrap and place in the freezer for 30 minutes or until the icing is firm. Remove from the freezer and spread with the remaining buttercream. Wrap firmly in plastic wrap to form a smooth ball shape and freeze for a further 30 minutes or until the icing is firm.

3   Meanwhile, for the bat, cut the rectangular cake in half lengthways, trim the ends and place end to end. Cut away about half of the top cake to form a handle, as shown *(pic 1)*. Using the rectangles cut from the handle, cut in half diagonally and

place along the centre of the bat, as shown, securing with a little brown buttercream *(pic 2)*. Trim to make a neat shape. Trim the corners off the top of the bat, near the handle, as shown.

4   Spread the brown buttercream all over the bat and handle. Coat the handle with the chocolate sprinkles. Remove the ball from the freezer and remove the plastic wrap immediately. Using the white writing gel, mark stitching lines around the ball and place next to the bat.

TIP: For this recipe you will need one quantity vanilla buttercake. Spoon ½ cup of the mixture into one greased 185 ml (6 fl oz/¾ cup) large (texas) cupcake/muffin tin hole and bake for 30 minutes. Spread the remaining cake mixture into a rectangular tin and bake for 30 minutes.

You will need a 35 cm x 60 cm (14 x 24 inch) rectangular cake board for this cake.

Use green-coloured coconut for grass on the board.

1   *Trim the end of one cake to form the handle of the bat.*

2   *Use the handle trim pieces to form the back of the bat.*

★ Space Explorer

Decorating Time: 1 hour 10 minutes

25 cm (10 inch) square
  vanilla buttercake (recipe
  page 142)
Space Explorer template
  (see template sheet)
1 quantity vanilla buttercream
  (recipe page 145)
Blue, orange, red and
  black food colourings
550 g (1 lb 4 oz) white
  fondant icing
Icing (confectioner's)
  sugar, sifted
2 small ice-cream cones
15 small silver cachous
  (edible silver balls)
45 yellow candy-coated
  fruit buttons

1 Use a sharp knife to level the top of the cake, if necessary. Place the cake on the board. Position the template for the rocket ship's body on the cake and secure with tooth-picks. Cut out around the body shape using a small sharp knife. Tint the buttercream using the blue food colouring to the desired colour. Spread the blue buttercream all over the rocket's body.

2 Tint 300 g (10½ oz) of the fondant icing using the orange food colouring to the desired colour. Tint 150 g (5½ oz) of the remaining fondant using the red food colouring to the desired colour. Tint the remaining fondant using the black food colouring. Knead all three fondants separately on a work surface lightly dusted with sifted icing sugar until smooth.

3 For the jet exhausts, use a serrated knife to trim the bottoms off the ice-cream cones. Gently press the cut ends into the tail of the rocket.

4 For the stripes and nose cone, roll the orange fondant on the work surface to about 4 mm (⅛ inch) thick. For the stripes, use a ruler and a knife and cut two 2 cm (¾ inch) wide strips out of

the fondant. Using the picture as a guide, position the orange strips on the rocket body.

5 For the nose cone, roll out the remaining orange fondant on the work surface to 3 mm (⅛ inch) thick. Cut out a triangle 15 × 15 × 25 cm (6 × 6 × 10 inch) and position on the tip of the rocket, moulding down the sides. Trim the edges and discard the trimmings.

6 For the wings, roll the red fondant on the work surface to about 5 mm (¼ inch) thick. Position the template for the wings on the fondant. Cut out around the shape of the wings using a small sharp knife. Position the wings on each side of the rocket and secure to the board with a little water.

7 For the star disk, roll out the black fondant on the work surface to 3 mm (⅛ inch) thick. Cut out a circle using a 5 cm (2 inch) round cutter. Stick onto the middle of the rocket body. Using star cutters cut out one small star and two larger stars from the remaining orange fondant.

8 Stick the larger stars on each wing and the small star on the black circle, securing with a little water. Using the picture as a guide, decorate the rocket with the silver cachous and yellow candy-coated fruit buttons.

You will need a 40 cm
(16 inch) square cake
board for this cake.

Use cardboard and/or fondant
icing to create flames, stars
and planets on the board.

Magic &
Enchantment

★ Princess Crown

Decorating Time: 1 hour 10 minutes

26 × 35 cm (10½ × 14 inch)
rectangular vanilla buttercake
(recipe page 142, see tip)

4 × 80 ml (2½ fl oz/⅓ cup)
vanilla cupcakes in paper
cases (see tip)

2 quantities vanilla buttercream
(recipe page 145)

Pink food colouring

Princess Crown template
(see template sheet)

5 purple round sugar-coated
jubes (gummy candies),
halved crossways

2 purple oval sugar-coated
jubes (gummy candies),
halved crossways

8 red round sugar-coated
jubes (gummy candies),
halved crossways

5 yellow triangle sugar-coated
jubes (gummy candies),
halved crossways

2 green triangle sugar-coated
jubes (gummy candies),
halved crossways

9 red candy-coated
chocolate chips

15 yellow candy-coated
chocolate chips

12 green candy-coated
chocolate chips

8 each purple and red
jellybeans

3 red sour straps or fruit
straps, cut into 5 mm
(¼ inch) wide strips

1 Use a sharp knife to level the
tops of the cakes, if necessary.
Tint the buttercream with the pink
food colouring to the desired colour.
Position the template on the cake
and secure with toothpicks. Cut out
around the crown shape using a
small sharp knife. Position the crown
on the cake board and secure with
a little of the buttercream.

2 Spread the pink buttercream all
over the large cake and the tops of
the small cakes. Using the picture
as a guide, position the small cakes
on the board above the crown.

3 Using the picture as a guide,
decorate the crown with the jubes
and candy-coated chocolate chips.
Decorate the small cakes in a
mosaic pattern with jellybeans
and the remaining jubes. Using
the picture as a guide, position
sour strap strips to outline the whole
crown and to form a headband.

TIP: For this recipe you will need
two quantities of vanilla buttercake.
Spoon ¼ cup of the mixture into each
of four greased 80 ml (2½ fl oz/⅓ cup)
cupcake/muffin tin holes and bake for
20–25 minutes. Spread the remaining
cake mixture into the rectangular tin
and bake for 50–55 minutes.

You will need a 40 cm
(16 inch) round cake board
for this cake.

Decorate the board with
a candy necklace.

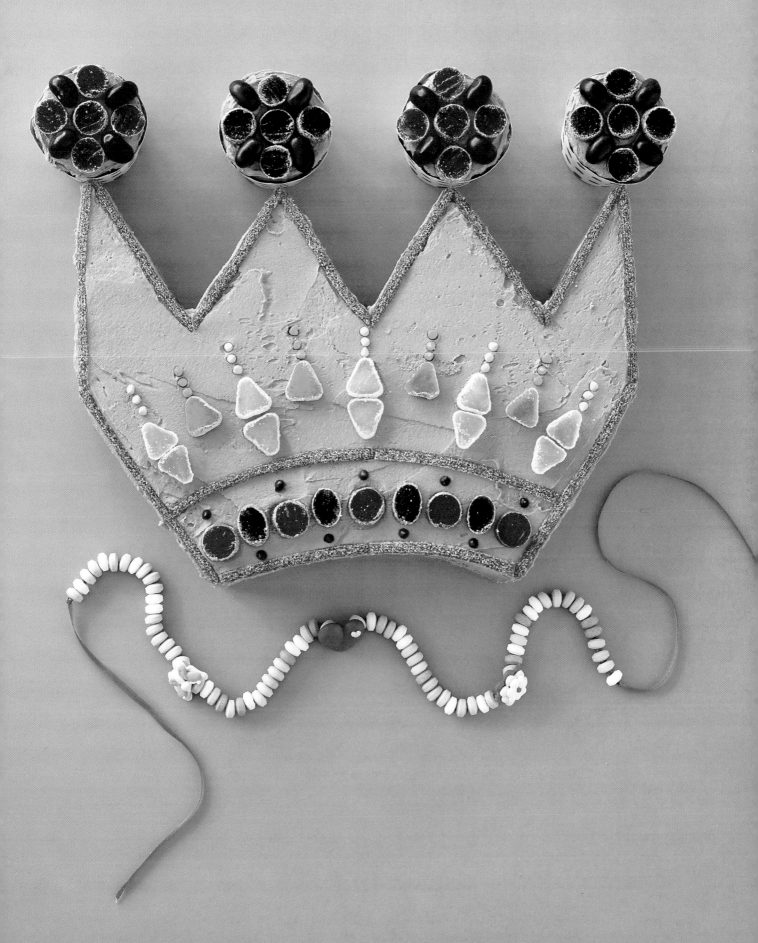

★ Rainbow Butterfly

Decorating Time: 1 hour 15 minutes

Two 20 × 30 cm (8 × 12 inch) rectangular vanilla buttercakes (recipe page 142)

2 quantities vanilla buttercream (recipe page 145)

Blue, yellow, pink, orange and green food colourings

Rainbow Butterfly template (see template sheet)

Coloured sprinkles

4 yellow round sugar-coated jubes (gummy candies), halved crossways

28 mini rock candies

4 pink round candies

2 purple round candies

10 cm (4 inch) black licorice strap

1 Use a sharp knife to level the tops of the cakes, if necessary. Divide the buttercream into five bowls, allowing slightly more in two of the bowls. Tint the larger bowls of buttercream with the blue and yellow food colourings to the desired colours. Tint the remaining three bowls with the pink, orange and green food colourings to the desired colours.

2 Place the cakes side by side on the work surface. Position the templates on the cakes and secure with toothpicks. Cut out around the butterfly shape using a small sharp knife. Using the picture as a guide, mark the pattern for the wings using a sharp knife.

3 Join the two body pieces with a little of the orange buttercream and spread orange buttercream all over the body. Carefully coat in the coloured sprinkles and set aside.

4 Place the remaining orange buttercream in a disposable piping (icing) bag and trim off the end. Using the picture as a guide, pipe squiggles all along one section of both wings. Repeat with the remaining coloured buttercreams to cover the wings. Using a small palette knife, spread matching buttercream around the sides of both wings.

5 Using the picture as a guide, decorate the wings with jubes and candies as shown. Place the wings and body on the cake board to create a butterfly. Cut two thin strips from the licorice and insert into the top of the body for the butterfly's antennae.

You will need a 40 cm (16 inch) square cake board for this cake.

Decorate the board with paper flowers.

★ Polly Dolly

Decorating Time: 1 hour 25 minutes

18 × 23 cm (7 × 9 inch) oval vanilla buttercake (recipe page 142)

1 quantity vanilla buttercream (recipe page 145)

375 g (13 oz) white fondant icing

Pink, yellow and black food colourings

Icing (confectioner's) sugar, sifted

Polly Dolly template (see template sheet)

2 × 40 cm (16 inch) striped ribbons, tied in bows

You will need a 25 x 30 cm (10 x 12 inch) oval cake board for this cake.

1 Use a sharp knife to level the top of the cake, if necessary. Position the cake on the cake board.

2 For the skin, tint the buttercream with the pink food colouring to the desired colour. Spread the pink buttercream over the top and sides of the cake, reserving a little buttercream to attach the ribbons.

3 For the hair, tint 250 g (9 oz) of the white fondant with the yellow food colouring to the desired colour. Knead the yellow fondant on a work surface lightly dusted with the sifted icing sugar until smooth. Roll on the work surface to 3 mm (⅛ inch) thick. Position the hair template on the fondant and cut out one hair shape. Flip the template and cut out another hair shape. Texture the fondant to create hair using the end of a paint-brush handle. To make plaits, divide the remaining yellow fondant into six equal pieces. Roll each piece into an 18 cm (7 inch) long sausage. Use three pieces to form one plait and repeat with the remaining three pieces. Using the picture as a guide, attach the hair and plaits to the cake using a little water.

4 For the eyes, roll 40 g (1½ oz) of the remaining white fondant on the work surface to 3 mm (⅛ inch) thick and cut out two 4 cm (1½ inch) ovals. For the pupils, tint 20 g (¾ oz) of the remaining fondant with the black food colouring. Knead the black fondant on a work surface lightly dusted with the sifted icing sugar until smooth. Roll on the work surface to 3 mm (⅛ inch) thick and cut out two 1 cm (½ inch) circles. Using the picture as a guide, position the white eyes on the cake, securing with a little water. Secure the black pupils with a little water.

5 Tint the remaining fondant with the pink food colouring to the desired colour. Knead the pink fondant on a work surface lightly dusted with the sifted icing sugar until smooth. For the nose, roll 15 g (½ oz) of the pink fondant into a ball. Secure to the face with a little water. For the cheeks, roll half of the remaining fondant on the work surface to 3 mm (⅛ inch) thick and cut out two 3 cm (1¼ inch) circles. Secure the cheeks to the face using a little water.

6 For the mouth, roll the remaining pink fondant into a thin sausage about 11 cm (4¼ inch) long and position on the cake, as shown. Attach a ribbon bow to each plait with a dab of reserved buttercream.

★ Fairy Garden

Decorating Time: 1 hour 15 minutes

8 × 20 cm (3¼ × 8 inch) vanilla buttercake, prepared in a nut roll tin (recipe page 142, see tip)

22 cm (8½ inch) round vanilla buttercake (recipe page 142, see tip)

1 quantity vanilla buttercream (recipe page 145)

2 tablespoons unsweetened cocoa powder, sifted

Green food colouring

350 g (12 oz) packet spearmint leaf-shaped sugar-coated jubes (gummy candies), halved lengthways

9 white rectangular mini hard candies

8 small flat lollipops

4 small fairy dolls

1 red mini candy-coated chocolate button

1 Use a sharp knife to level the tops of the cakes, if necessary. Combine ½ cup of the vanilla buttercream and the cocoa in a small bowl. Tint the remaining buttercream with the green food colouring to the desired colour.

2 Position the round cake in the centre of the cake board. Position the nut roll cake upright, off-centre on top of the round cake. Secure to the round cake by pushing three bamboo skewers through the cakes (remove the skewers before serving).

3 Spread the green buttercream all over the round cake. Spread the chocolate buttercream all over the nut roll cake. Rough up the chocolate buttercream using a spatula to resemble tree bark.

4 Using the picture as a guide, decorate the cake with the halved spearmint leaves, mini hard candies, lollipops and fairies. Remove the stick from one lollipop and position the top as a door. Discard the stick. Position the red mini candy-coated chocolate button on the lollipop door, securing with a little buttercream.

TIP: For this recipe you will need two quantities of vanilla buttercake. Spoon one-quarter of the double quantity into a nut roll tin and bake for 1 hour 10 minutes. Spread the remaining cake mixture into a 22 cm (8½ inch) round cake tin and bake for 1 hour.

You will need a 30 cm (12 inch) round cake board for this cake.

★ Glambag

Decorating Time: 1 hour 25 minutes

Two 9 × 19 cm (3½ × 7½ inch)
loaf vanilla buttercakes
(recipe page 142)
1½ quantities vanilla
buttercream (recipe
page 145)
Purple food colouring
7 pink candy sticks
**44 candy-coated
fruit buttons**
**2 yellow triangle sugar-
coated jubes (gummy
candies)**
14 sugar flowers (see tip)
**30 cm (12 inch) red
licorice twist**

1 Use a sharp knife to level the tops of the cakes, if necessary. Tint the buttercream with the purple food colouring to the desired colour.

2 Cut the cakes in half horizontally. Place the loaf cakes on the cake board, on top of each other, joining with a little buttercream. Using a serrated knife, trim the top and sides of the cake stack to form a handbag shape.

3 Spread the purple buttercream all over the cake. Using the picture as a guide, decorate the handbag with the candies.

4 Press the licorice twist into the top of the cake to create a handle. Mark stitching lines around the edges of the cake with a fork.

TIP: Sugar flowers are small flowers made from fondant icing. They are available in the cake decorating section of most supermarkets.

You will need a 22 cm (8½ inch) square cake board for this cake.

★ Spotty Dotty

Decorating Time: 1 hour 15 minutes

2 × 25 cm (10 inch) round
chocolate mud cakes
(recipe page 144)
1 quantity dark chocolate
ganache (recipe page 149)
1.5 kg (3 lb 5 oz) white
fondant icing
Yellow, pink, blue, orange
and green food colourings
Icing (confectioner's)
sugar, sifted

1 Use a sharp knife to level the tops of the cakes, if necessary. Place the ganache in a medium bowl and whisk for 30 seconds or until soft and fluffy. Place one cake upside down on the cake board and secure with a little ganache. Spread a thin layer of ganache over the cake, sandwich with the remaining cake, also upside down. Spread the remaining ganache all over the cake, smoothing the surface with a spatula. Refrigerate until set.

2 Tint 100 g (3½ oz) of the white fondant with the yellow food colouring, 100 g (3½ oz) with the pink food colouring, 100 g (3½ oz) with the blue food colouring and 100 g (3½ oz) with the orange food colouring to the desired colours. Tint the remaining fondant with the green food colouring to the desired colour. Knead each colour fondant on a work surface lightly dusted with the sifted icing sugar until smooth.

3 Roll out the yellow, pink, blue and orange fondants separately on the work surface to 5 mm (¼ inch) thick. Using a set of different sized round cutters (see tip), cut out different sized spots from each of the different coloured fondants. Place the circles of fondant on a tray and cover with plastic wrap to prevent them from drying out. Wrap the fondant trimmings and reserve for the balls.

4 Roll out the green fondant on the work surface into a round 1.5 cm (⅝ inch) thick. Using a paintbrush and a little water, stick the prepared cut-out spots randomly all over the rolled-out green fondant. Then continue rolling out the fondant round until it is 5 mm (¼ inch) thick and the spots appear flat. Using a rolling pin, gently lift the fondant over the cake. Using warm dry hands, gently smooth the fondant down over the sides. Trim off any excess fondant around the base of the cake and smooth all over with the palm of your hands.

5 To finish, roll different sized balls of each of the reserved coloured fondant trimmings using your hands. Use a paintbrush and a little water to stick them around the bottom edge.

TIP: We used 3, 4 and 5 cm (1, 1½ and 2 inch) cutters for the spots.

You will need a 30 cm (12 inch) round cake board for this cake.

Use a pin to prick and remove any air bubbles that may appear under the fondant before smoothing with the palm of your hand.

★ Princess Castle

Decorating Time: 1 hour 10 minutes

2 × 25 cm (10 inch) square vanilla buttercakes (recipe page 142)

2 × 20 cm (8 inch) round vanilla buttercakes (recipe page 142)

3 quantities vanilla buttercream (recipe page 145)

Green and pink food colourings

100 g (3½ oz) pink and white mini marshmallows

2 × 15 g (½ oz) white chocolate bars

10 red mini candy-coated chocolate buttons

Four 12 × 20 cm (4½ × 8 inch) pink cardboard rectangles

Four 15 cm (6 inch) diameter circles of pink glitter cardboard

4 paper flags on toothpicks

Six 55 cm (2½ × 22 inch) rectangles of pink glitter cardboard

Four 4 cm (1½ inch) pieces patterned tape

1 Use a sharp knife to level the tops of the cakes, if necessary. Cut the corners from both the square cakes to make octagon shapes.

2 Tint ¼ cup of the buttercream with the green food colouring to the desired colour. Tint the remaining buttercream with the pink food colouring to desired colour. Reserve ¼ cup of the pink buttercream.

3 Sandwich the two octagon-shaped cakes with a little of the pink buttercream. Place on the centre of the cake board, securing with a little buttercream. Spread the top and sides of the cake with the pink buttercream. Sandwich the two round cakes with a little of the pink buttercream. Place the round cakes on top of the octagon cake. Spread the top and sides of the round cakes with pink buttercream.

4 Using a piping (icing) bag fitted with a 5 mm (¼ inch) round tip, pipe small rounds of reserved pink buttercream around the top edges of each cake. Using the picture as a guide, decorate the cake with the mini marshmallows.

5 For the doors, position the white chocolate bars on the cake, as shown. Using a little buttercream position one red mini candy-coated chocolate button on each door to make handles. Using a piping (icing) bag fitted with a 2 mm (¹⁄₁₆ inch) round piping tip, pipe green buttercream on the walls of the cake for ivy. Position the remaining red mini candy-coated chocolate buttons on the ivy to make flowers.

6 For the towers, make four cylinders out of the pink cardboard rectangles, securing with tape and position at the corners of the cake. Make four cone shapes out of the glitter cardboard circles, cutting a slit into the centre and securing with tape. Sit on top of the cardboard towers. Insert the flags into the tops of the towers. Attach a piece of tape to each tower to make the windows. Using scissors, cut a rampart pattern along one edge of the glitter cardboard rectangle. Staple the ends of the rectangle together to form a ring. Position the rampart ring on top of the cake.

You will need a 40 cm (16 inch) square cake board for this cake.

★ Sea Princess

Decorating Time: 1 hour 30 minutes

2.5 litre (10 cup) vanilla buttercake, prepared in a dolly varden tin (recipe page 142, see tips)

18 × 40 ml (1¼ fl oz) vanilla cupcakes in silver foil cases (see tips)

1½ quantities vanilla buttercream (recipe page 145)

Yellow and blue food colourings

1 tablespoon almond meal (ground almonds) (see tips)

28 cm (11¼ inch) tall doll, (remove legs)

6 each green and yellow round sugar-coated jubes (gummy candies)

1 spearmint leaf-shaped sugar-coated jube (gummy candy), halved lengthways

3 rainbow sour straps or fruit straps

1 Use a sharp knife to level the tops of the cakes, if necessary. Tint ⅓ cup of the buttercream with the yellow food colouring to the desired colour. Reserve ¼ cup of the uncoloured buttercream for the waves. Tint the remaining buttercream with the blue food colouring to the desired colour.

2 Position the large cake, upside down, in the centre of the cake board, securing with a little of the blue buttercream. Using a teaspoon, scoop a hole from the top of cake deep enough to fit the body of the doll.

3 Spread the blue buttercream all over the large cake and the tops of the small cakes. Using a spatula, swirl the reserved uncoloured buttercream into the blue buttercream on the small cakes and around the base of the large cake to create waves.

4 Spread the yellow buttercream on the board around the large cake, then sprinkle with the almond meal to create sand (see tips). Gently push the doll into the cake to waist level.

5 Using a sharp knife, cut the jubes in half crossways. Then cut each piece in half again to make half circles.

Using the picture as a guide, arrange the jubes in the shape of a mermaid's tail down the front of the large cake. Position the two spearmint leaves at the end of the tail.

6 Remove the green section from the rainbow sour straps, then halve crossways. Using the picture as a guide, twist each piece of green strap and position on the cake to create seaweed. Arrange the cupcakes randomly around the board.

TIPS: For this recipe you will need three quantities of vanilla buttercake. Spoon 1 level tablespoon of the mixture into each of 18 greased 40 ml (1¼ fl oz) foil cases and bake for 10–15 minutes. Spread the remaining cake mixture into the dolly varden tin and bake for 1 hour 15 minutes.

Do NOT use almond meal if any party guests are allergic to nuts or seeds. Use coloured sugar instead.

You will need a 30 cm (12 inch) round cake board for this cake.

Adventure & Imagination

★ Crazy Clown

Decorating Time: 1 hour 30 minutes

20 cm (8 inch) round vanilla buttercake (recipe page 142, see tip)

23 cm (9 inch) square vanilla buttercake (recipe page 142, see tip)

1 × 40 ml (1¼ fl oz) vanilla cupcake (see tip)

2 quantities vanilla buttercream (recipe page 145)

Red, yellow, green and pink food colourings

Crazy Clown template (see template sheet)

Red and black writing gels

4 marshmallows

1 yellow candy stick

2 pink candy sticks

10 candy-coated chocolate buttons

Fairy floss (cotton candy)

You will need a 30 cm (12 inch) round cake board for this cake.

1 Use a sharp knife to level the tops of the cakes, if necessary. Set aside 1 tablespoon of the vanilla buttercream for the mouth. Tint 2 tablespoons of the buttercream with the red food colouring to the desired colour. Tint ½ cup of the remaining buttercream with the yellow colouring to the desired colour. Divide the remaining buttercream into two portions. Tint one portion green and the remaining portion pale pink.

2 For the nose, trim the cupcake into a half ball shape and spread with half the red buttercream. Wrap in plastic wrap and place in the freezer to firm. When firm, remove from the freezer and spread with the remaining red buttercream. Wrap firmly in plastic wrap to form a smooth shape and freeze again to firm. Remove from the freezer and peel off the plastic wrap immediately. Set aside.

3 Meanwhile, using a serrated knife, cut a 3 cm (1¼ inch) slice off one side of the round buttercake to create a flat edge for the clown's hat to sit on. Spread the pink buttercream over the top and sides of the round cake.

4 For the hat and collar, position the hat and collar templates on the square cake and secure with toothpicks. Cut out around the clown's hat and collar

shapes using a small sharp knife. Spread the green buttercream over the triangle (hat) shape. Using a spatula or knife, make stroke marks in the buttercream to create stripes on the hat. Position the hat at the top of the head. Spread the yellow buttercream over the collar shape and attach under the head.

5 Carefully spread the reserved uncoloured buttercream in a curved shape for the mouth. Using the picture as a guide, outline the lips and mouth using the red writing gel. Using the black writing gel, draw eyes and eyebrows. Decorate the hat with the marshmallows and the yellow candy stick. Decorate the collar with lengths of the pink candy sticks and the candy-coated chocolate buttons. Place the nose in the centre of the cake and position the fairy floss for the hair.

TIP: For this recipe you will need two quantities of vanilla buttercake. Spoon 1½ tablespoons of the mixture into one greased 40 ml (1¼ fl oz) cupcake/muffin hole and bake for 10–15 minutes. Divide the remaining cake mixture evenly between the prepared round and square tins and bake the round cake for 45–50 minutes and the square cake for 1 hour 10 minutes.

★ Chocolate Crackle Cake

Decorating Time: 1 hour 10 minutes

60 g (2¼ oz/2 cups) puffed
  rice cereal
40 g (1½ oz/½ cup)
  shredded coconut
200 g (7 oz/1⅓ cups) milk
  chocolate melts, melted
Coloured sprinkles
2 × 22 cm (8½ inch) round
  vanilla buttercakes (recipe
  page 142, see tip)
1 quantity vanilla
  buttercream (recipe
  page 145)
Pink food colouring
7.5 × 120 cm (3 × 47 inch)
  piece of baking paper
  (parchment)
7.5 × 120 cm (3 × 47 inch)
  piece of pink and white
  striped paper

1 Combine the puffed rice cereal
and coconut in a large mixing bowl.
Add the melted chocolate and stir well
to combine. Place heaped tablespoons
of the mixture in small piles on a tray
lined with baking paper. Mould each
tablespoon of the mixture into a neat
mound. Sprinkle with the coloured
sprinkles. Stand for 20 minutes or
until set.

2 Meanwhile, use a sharp knife to
level the tops of the cakes, if necessary.
Tint the buttercream with the pink
food colouring to the desired colour.
Sandwich the cakes with a little of the
buttercream. Using a serrated knife,
trim the side of the whole cake at a
slight angle to taper down and form
a cupcake shape.

3 Spread the cake all over with the
remaining buttercream. Pile the set
chocolate crackles on top of the cake.

4 Place the baking paper on top of
the decorative paper. Fold the paper
stack back and forth in 2 cm (¾ inch)
wide sections as if making a paper fan.
Wrap the paper, baking paper side in,
around the edge of the cake to create
a cupcake paper case, secure with
tape. Decorate with candles.

TIP: For this recipe you will need two
quantities of the vanilla buttercake.
Divide the mixture between each
cake tin and bake for both for
45–50 minutes.

You will need a 30 cm
(12 inch) round cake
board for this cake.

★ Treasure Chest

Decorating Time: 1 hour 20 minutes

Three 9 × 19 cm (3½ × 7½ inch) loaf vanilla buttercakes (recipe page 142)

2 quantities chocolate buttercream (recipe page 145)

5 × 80 g (2¾ oz) packets chocolate gold coins

58 chocolate-coated finger biscuits (cookies)

4 green round sugar-coated jubes (gummy candies), halved crossways

4 red round sugar-coated jubes (gummy candies), halved crossways

1 Use a sharp knife to level the tops of the cakes, if necessary. Position one cake on the cake board. Cut one rectangle of cake about 15 × 5 cm (6 × 2 inch) and 3 cm (1¼ inch) deep from the centre of one of the remaining cakes leaving a 2 cm (¾ inch) rim around the edge, as shown. Position on top of the cake to make the base of the treasure chest (pic 1).

2 For the lid, trim the remaining loaf cake to fit the base of the chest and check the position so that it fits neatly, as shown (pic 2).

3 Cover the top and sides of the treasure chest base with the chocolate buttercream. Cover the lid with the chocolate buttercream. Fill the chest with the gold coins. Position the lid on top of the chest.

4 Using the picture as a guide, position the chocolate-coated finger biscuits on the treasure chest and lid. Position the jube halves on the chest to represent jewels.

You will need a 25 cm (10 inch) round cake board for this cake.

1 *Cut out a rectangle from the middle of one cake to form the chest.*

2 *Check the size and position of the lid before covering in buttercream.*

★ Jolly Pirate

Decorating Time: 1 hour 30 minutes

18 × 23 cm (7 × 9 in) oval vanilla buttercake (recipe page 142)

1 quantity vanilla buttercream (recipe page 145)

800 g (1 lb 12 oz) white fondant icing

Pink, red, yellow, black and brown food colourings

Icing (confectioner's) sugar, sifted

Jolly Pirate template (see template sheet)

25 cm (10 inch) black licorice strap

You will need a 23 x 28 cm (9 x 11¼ inch) oval cake board for this cake.

1 Use a sharp knife to level the top of the cake, if necessary. Position the cake on the cake board and spread the buttercream all over the cake.

2 For the pirate's skin, tint 440 g (15½ oz) of the fondant icing with the food colouring to the desired colour. Knead the skin-coloured fondant on a work surface lightly dusted with the sifted icing sugar until smooth. Roll on the work surface to 5 mm (¼ inch) thick and large enough to cover the cake. Using a rolling pin, gently lift the fondant onto the cake. Using warm dry hands, gently smooth the fondant over the cake. Trim off any excess around the base of the cake. Roll the trimmings into a small smooth ball and reserve for the nose.

3 For the scarf, tint 140 g (5 oz) of the remaining fondant with the red food colouring to the desired colour. Knead the red fondant on a work surface lightly dusted with the sifted icing sugar until smooth. Roll on the work surface to 5 mm (¼ inch) thick. Tint 60 g (2 oz) of the remaining fondant with the yellow food colouring to the desired colour. Roll small pieces of the yellow fondant into balls. Flatten the balls and attach randomly to the red fondant with a little water. Roll the fondant all over very gently to make sure the spots are secure and to create a smooth spotted-fabric effect. Using the picture as a guide, attach to the top

of the face as a scarf, securing with a little water. Trim to size and mould the trimmings to form a tied knot.

4 For the pirate's eye, roll 40 g (1½ oz) of the remaining white fondant on the work surface to 3 mm (⅛ inch) thick and cut out a 4 cm (1½ inch) oval. Also cut two rectangles for the teeth.

5 Tint 80 g (2¾ oz) of the remaining fondant with black food colouring. Knead the black fondant on a work surface lightly dusted with the sifted icing sugar until smooth. Roll on the work surface to 3 mm (⅛ inch) thick and cut out a 1 cm (½ inch) circle for the pupil. Using the mouth and eye patch templates, cut out the mouth and patch shapes from the black icing.

6 Using the picture as a guide, position the white eye on the cake, securing with a little water. Secure the black pupil with a little water. Secure the mouth, teeth, eye patch and reserved nose with a little water. Cut a thin strip from the licorice strap and position around the head to create the band for the eye patch.

7 For the tufts of hair, tint the remaining fondant with the food colouring to the desired colour. Mould short pointed shapes and attach to the head using a little water. Using a fine paintbrush, paint small dots of food colouring onto the face as stubble.

★ The Giant Slice

Decorating Time: 1 hour 30 minutes

2 × 25 cm (10 inch) square
chocolate mud cakes
(recipe page 144)

**The Giant Slice template
(see template sheet)**

1½ quantities dark chocolate
ganache (recipe page 149)

1 quantity vanilla buttercream
(recipe page 145)

Pink, yellow, blue and red
food colourings

½ quantity vanilla glace icing
(recipe page 148)

100 g (3½ oz) white
fondant icing

2 tablespoons candy-coated
chocolate chips

*You will need a 30 cm
(12 inch) round cake
board for this cake.*

1 Use a sharp knife to level the tops of the cakes, if necessary. Position the cake template on one half of one of the cakes. Using a sharp knife, cut out one slice shape. Position the template on the other half of the cake and cut out a second slice shape. Position the template on the remaining cake and cut out a third slice shape.

2 Place the ganache in a medium bowl and whisk for 30 seconds or until soft and fluffy. Position the first layer (slice) of cake on the cake board, securing with a little ganache. Spread a thin layer of ganache on the first layer of cake. Top with a second layer (slice) of cake. Repeat the layers with a little more ganache using the third layer (slice) of cake. Spread the remaining ganache over the top and sides of the cake. Smooth the ganache with a palette knife or spatula. Refrigerate for 30 minutes or until set.

3 Tint three-quarters of the buttercream with the pink food colouring to the desired colour. Tint the remaining buttercream with the yellow food colouring to the desired colour. Reserve 2 tablespoons of each colour buttercream for the cake filling. Tint the reserved pink buttercream with the red food colouring to the desired colour. Tint the glace icing with the blue food colouring to the desired colour. Cover with plastic wrap to prevent it forming a skin.

4 Spread the pink buttercream over the top and back of the cake slice. Using a piping (icing) bag fitted with a 1 cm (½ inch) plain tip, pipe a shell edge of the yellow buttercream at the base of the back of the cake slice. Using a piping bag fitted with a 5 mm (¼ inch) plain tip, pipe a line of the reserved yellow buttercream and then a line of the reserved red buttercream along the centre on each side of the slice of cake, as shown, to represent the filling in the cake.

5 For the candle, tint 80 g (2¾ oz) of the fondant with the blue food colouring to the desired colour. Using your hands, roll the blue fondant into a 2 × 10 cm (¾ × 4 inch) candle. Insert a 15 cm (6 inch) wooden skewer through the centre of the candle to give it stability. Tint half of the remaining fondant red and the other half yellow. Marble the fondants together into a teardrop shape. Sit on the top of the skewer to resemble the candle's flame. Set aside to dry.

6 For the top icing, pour the blue glace icing over the top of the cake very slowly, pushing it towards the edge with a tablespoon so that a little drizzles down the sides of the cake. Stick the candle into the top of the cake and scatter candy-coated chocolate chips over the glace icing.

★ Daisy Cake

Decorating Time: 1 hour 10 minutes + overnight drying

2 × 30 cm (12 inch) round
vanilla buttercakes (recipe
page 142)

3 quantities vanilla
buttercream (recipe
page 145)

Yellow food colouring

250 g (9 oz) white
fondant icing

Icing (confectioner's)
sugar, sifted

200 g (7 oz) bought
lemon curd

250 ml (9 fl oz/1 cup) thick
cream, whipped to firm
peaks

1 Use a sharp knife to level the tops of the cakes, if necessary. Tint the buttercream with the yellow food colouring to the desired colour.

2 Knead the fondant icing on a work surface lightly dusted with the sifted icing sugar until smooth. Roll on the work surface to 2 mm (1/16 inch) thick. Using a 4 cm (1½ inch) flower cutter, cut out 20 flowers. Using a 3 cm (1¼ inch) flower cutter, cut out 30 flowers. Using a 2 cm (¾ inch) flower cutter, cut out 50 flowers. Shape the flowers by pressing them into the palm of your hand and gently curving the petals upwards. Set aside to dry overnight.

3 To decorate, position one cake on the cake board. Spread with the lemon curd and then the whipped cream and sandwich with the remaining cake, upside down. Spread the top and sides of the whole cake with two-thirds of the yellow buttercream.

4 Using the picture as a guide, position two-thirds of the different sized flowers on the cake in the shape of a heart. Position the remaining flowers around the side of the cake. Using a piping (icing) bag fitted with a 2 mm (1/16 inch) round piping tip, pipe a dot of the remaining yellow buttercream into the centre of each flower.

You will need a 40 cm
(16 inch) round cake
board for this cake.

★ ABC Cakes

Decorating Time: 1 hour 20 minutes

36 × 80 ml (2½ fl oz/⅓ cup) vanilla cupcakes (recipe page 142, see tip)

320 g (11¼ oz/1 cup) raspberry jam, warmed, strained

1 kg (2 lb 4 oz) white fondant icing

Icing (confectioner's) sugar, sifted

Red, orange, yellow and blue food colourings

20 g (¾ oz) white fondant icing, extra

4 cm (1½ inch) black licorice strap, cut into thirds lengthways

1 rainbow sour strap or fruit strap

1 grape mini jube (gumdrop)

2 ice-cream shaped soft candies

1 pig-shaped soft candy

1 shell chocolate

2 × 35 g (1¼ oz) tubes mini candy-coated chocolate buttons

1 each butterfly and heart icing decorations

3 flower icing decorations

1 crown icing decoration

1 coloured paper cocktail umbrella

1   Use a sharp knife to level the tops of the cupcakes, if necessary. Brush a thin layer of jam over the top of the cakes.

2   Knead the fondant icing on a work surface lightly dusted with the sifted icing sugar until smooth. Divide the fondant into four portions. Tint one portion red, another orange, another yellow and the remaining portion blue using the food colourings to the desired colours.

3   Roll out the red fondant on the work surface to 3 mm (⅛ inch) thick. Using a 6 cm (2½ inch) round cutter, cut out 12 rounds. Position the rounds on top of 12 cakes. Repeat with the orange and yellow fondant and the remaining cakes. Using the picture as a guide, place the cakes on the cake board.

4   For the zebra stripes, roll the extra white fondant on the work surface to 5 mm (¼ inch) thick. Cut one 5 mm × 4 cm (¼ × 1½ inch) strip from the fondant; discard any excess. Brush the top of the letter Z cake with a little water. Using the picture as a guide, top with white fondant and two of the licorice strips. Discard the remaining licorice.

You will need a 45 cm (17¾ inch) round cake board for this cake.

5 For the letters, roll out the blue fondant on the work surface to 3 mm (⅛ inch) thick. Using letter cutters, cut out each letter of the alphabet. Brush the back of each letter with a little water and position on the cakes.

6 For the kite, cut a diamond shape from one end of the sour strap. Cut a thin strip of one colour from the other end of the sour strap. Using the picture as a guide, cut and attach thin strips of sour strap to the diamond shape using a little jam. Position the kite on the letter K cake with a little water, then add a strip of sour strap for the tail, as shown.

7 Using the picture as a guide, decorate the cakes with the remaining candies, decorations and umbrella, securing with a little water.

TIP: Cakes can be covered with buttercream instead of fondant. You will need two quantities of buttercream (recipe page 145).

★ Gift Box

Decorating Time: 1 hour 20 minutes + refrigeration

Two 20 × 30 cm (8 × 12 inch)
 rectangular mudcakes
 (recipe page 144)
1 quantity chocolate
 ganache, softened
 (recipe page 149)
1 kg (2 lb 4 oz) white
 fondant icing
Icing (confectioner's)
 sugar, sifted
Pink food colouring
Butterfly stencil (available
 at craft suppliers)
1.5 m (60 inch) pink
 satin ribbon

1   Use a sharp knife to level the tops of the cakes and trim sides, if necessary. Cut each cake in half vertically to make four rectangles. Stack the four cake pieces on top of each other, sandwiching with a little ganache between each layer. Trim the edges to make a neat block shape. Spread the remaining ganache all over the cake. Refrigerate for 30 minutes, or until the ganache is set.

2   Knead the fondant on a work surface lightly dusted with sifted icing sugar until smooth. Roll on the work surface to make a rectangle shape about 5 mm (¼ inch) thick. Using a rolling pin, gently lift the fondant onto the cake. Using warm dry hands, smooth the fondant over the top of the cake allowing it to drape gently down the sides. Ease the fondant in and down the sides. Fold the short sides like wrapping a paper present. Trim off any excess around the base and smooth all over with the palms of your hands to create a flat surface.

3   Dip a sponge or small paintbrush in the pink food colouring, blotting off any excess on kitchen paper. Holding the stencil gently against the cake and dab lightly with the sponge or brush. Carefully remove the stencil and repeat all over the cake. Allow to dry.

4   Cut two pieces of ribbon, one slightly longer than the length of the cake and one slightly longer than the width of the cake. Place one length of ribbon over the length of the cake and the other over the width. Using the point of a knife, poke the ribbon ends gently under the bottom edges of the cake. Make a bow from the remaining ribbon and attach to the top of the cake using double-sided tape. Add a gift tag with a greeting, if desired.

TIP: Use a soft paintbrush with a flat straight end or a piece of sponge (available at craft suppliers) for applying the stencil. Choose a stencil pattern appropriate to the occasion. (Instructions for stencilling are on page 157.)

You will need a 25 cm (10 inch) square cake board for this cake.

★ Parachuting Penny

Decorating Time: 1 hour 15 minutes

24 cm (9½ inch) round
  vanilla buttercake
  (recipe page 142)
Parachuting Penny template
  (see template sheet)
1½ quantities vanilla
  buttercream (recipe
  page 145)
Orange, red, yellow and
  green food colourings
50 cm (20 inch) black
  licorice strap
5 black pipe cleaners
Small doll or teddy

1 Using a serrated knife, cut the edge off one side of the top of the cake to make it slightly taper away, giving a rounded look to the top of the parachute. Position the template on the cake and secure with toothpicks. Cut out around the parachute shape using a small sharp knife.

2 Divide the buttercream into four bowls, putting slightly more in two of the bowls. Tint the larger bowls of buttercream with the orange and red food colourings to the desired colours. Tint the remaining two bowls with the yellow and green food colourings to the desired colours.

3 Using the picture as a guide, mark the sections on the cake for the parachute stripes with a sharp knife. Spread a different colour buttercream on each of the sections.

4 Cut the licorice strap into long thin strips and position on the cake to outline the parachute and separate the colours. Use the pipe cleaners as parachute strings. Add a small doll or teddy as the parachutist.

You will need a 25 x 35 cm (10 x 14 inch) round cake board for this cake.

Use red, white and black felt for the target on the board.

One-Hour Wonders

★ Waterbaby

Decorating Time: 1 hour

26 × 35 cm (10½ × 14 inch) rectangular vanilla buttercake (recipe page 142)

1 quantity vanilla buttercream (recipe page 145)

Pink food colouring

Waterbaby template (see template sheet)

250 g (9 oz) white fondant icing

Icing (confectioner's) sugar, sifted

86 red mini candy-coated chocolate buttons

68 green mini candy-coated chocolate buttons

73 blue mini candy-coated chocolate buttons

66 orange mini candy-coated chocolate buttons

1 Use a sharp knife to level the top of the cake, if necessary. Tint the buttercream using the pink food colouring to the desired colour. Position the swimsuit template on the cake and secure with toothpicks. Cut out around the swimsuit shape using a small sharp knife. Discard the excess cake.

2 Position the swimsuit on the cake board, securing with a little of the buttercream. Spread the buttercream all over the cake.

3 Knead the fondant icing on a work surface lightly dusted with the sifted icing sugar until smooth. Divide the fondant in half. Roll out one portion on the work surface to 5 mm (¼ inch) thick. Using the leg hole templates, cut out the two oval shapes to represent the leg holes. Using the picture as a guide, position the oval shapes on the cake.

4 Roll the remaining fondant on the work surface to an 8 × 40 cm (3¼ × 16 inch) rectangle. Cut one 1.5 × 5 cm (⅝ × 2 inch) strip, two 1.5 cm × 30 cm (⅝ × 12 inch) strips and one 2.5 × 40 cm (1 × 16 inch) strip from the fondant.

5 Using the picture as a guide, position the 1.5 × 5 cm strip across the top of the swimsuit. Then position one 1.5 cm × 30 cm strip around one armhole, trim and tuck the ends of the strip under the cake. Repeat with the remaining 1.5 cm × 30 cm strip on the other armhole. Use the two trimmed lengths to form a cross-over at the back for the straps.

6 Using the picture as a guide, ruffle the remaining 2.5 × 40 cm strip and position it across the front of the cake. Decorate the cake with rows of the mini candy-coated chocolate buttons, as shown.

You will need a 45 cm (17¾ inch) square cake board for this cake.

★ Juicy Watermelon

Decorating Time: 1 hour

30 cm (12 inch) round vanilla buttercake (recipe page 142)

2 quantities vanilla buttercream (recipe page 145)

Pink, red and green food colourings

24 brown mini candy-coated chocolate buttons

1 Use a sharp knife to level the top of the cake, if necessary. Tint 1½ cups of the buttercream with a mixture of the pink and red food colourings to resemble the colour of watermelon flesh. Tint ¾ cup of the buttercream with the green food colouring to the desired colour of watermelon skin. Leave the remaining buttercream uncoloured.

2 Place the cake on the board. Using the picture as a guide, cut the cake two-thirds of the way through to make one large watermelon piece (this piece is 16 cm/6¼ inch at its widest point). Cut the remaining cake into a second watermelon wedge (this wedge is 12 cm/4½ inch at its widest point). Discard any remaining cake.

3 Spread the green buttercream over the rounded edge of each watermelon piece to make the skin. Add dots of uncoloured buttercream about 3 cm (1¼ inch) apart over the green buttercream and use a spatula to swirl into the green buttercream to create a speckled look of the skin.

4 Spread the remaining cake with the watermelon-coloured buttercream. Press the mini candy-coated chocolate buttons sideways into the watermelon flesh to create the seeds.

You will need a 36 cm (14¼ inch) round cake board for this cake.

★ Yellow Kite

Decorating Time: 1 hour

26 × 35 cm (10½ × 14 inch) rectangular vanilla buttercake (recipe page 142)

2 quantities vanilla buttercream (recipe page 145)

Yellow Kite template (see template sheet)

Yellow, red and black food colourings

100 g (3½ oz) white fondant icing

Icing (confectioner's) sugar, sifted

1 blue sour strap or fruit strap

Black writing gel

50 cm (20 inch) × 3 cm (1¼ inch) wide white rope

1 m (40 inch) × 1 cm (½ inch) wide each of red, blue, green and striped ribbons

1 Use a sharp knife to level the top of the cake, if necessary. Position the template on the cake and secure with toothpicks. Using a serrated knife, cut out around the kite shape. Position the cake on the board, cut side down. Discard the remaining cake. Tint the buttercream with the yellow food colouring to the desired colour. Spread the buttercream all over the top and sides of the cake. Use a spatula to create a striped pattern in the buttercream.

2 For the eyes, roll out 20 g (¾ oz) of fondant icing on a work surface lightly dusted with sifted icing sugar to 3 mm (⅛ inch) thick. Cut out two 4 × 3 cm (1½ × 1¼ inch) oval shapes for eyes. Using the picture as a guide, attach to the cake using a little water.

3 Tint 40 g (1½ oz) of the remaining fondant with the red food colouring to the desired colour. Use the red fondant to mould the nose and the tongue. Tint the remaining fondant with the black food colouring and mould the mouth and pupils.

4 Trim and attach the sour straps to make a cross on the kite. Position and attach the face pieces, using a little water. Pipe the corners of the mouth and the eyebrows with the black writing gel. Using the coloured ribbons, tie a bow around the rope and position on the board at the base of the kite, as shown.

You will need a 40 x 50 cm (16 x 20 inch) rectangular cake board for this cake.

★ Magic Wand

Decorating Time: 1 hour

25 cm (10 inch) square
  vanilla buttercake (recipe
  page 142)

1 quantity vanilla
  buttercream (recipe
  page 145)

Pink food colouring

Magic Wand template
  (see template sheet)

30 × 1 cm diameter
  (12 × ½ inch) wooden
  stick

1.5 m (60 inch) × 1 cm
  (½ inch) wide pink
  striped ribbon

53 pink ice-cream shaped
  soft candies

35 yellow ice-cream shaped
  soft candies

1 Use a sharp knife to level the top of the cake, if necessary. Tint the buttercream using the pink food colouring to the desired colour. Position the template on the cake and secure with toothpicks. Using a serrated knife, cut out around the wand shape. Position the cake on the board, upside down, securing with a little buttercream. Cut a small amount of cake from the bottom star point to make a flat edge to insert the stick. Discard the cake offcuts. Spread the buttercream over the top and sides of the cake.

2 For the wand handle, wrap 1 metre (40 inch) of the ribbon around the stick. Tie the remainder of the ribbon in a bow around the top of the stick. Position the stick in the bottom of the cake.

3 Position the pink and yellow ice-cream shaped candies on the cake working from the outside in to make a star.

TIP: The cake can be sprinkled with silver or pink edible glitter, available from speciality cake decorating suppliers.

You will need a 36 cm
(14¼ inch) round cake
board for this cake.

★ Hello Sunshine

Decorating Time: 1 hour

Two 20 × 30 cm (8 × 12 inch)
rectangular vanilla
buttercakes (recipe
page 142)

2 quantities vanilla
buttercream (recipe
page 145)

Hello Sunshine template
(see template sheet)

Yellow and orange
food colourings

2 white marshmallows

2 red jellybeans

Black writing gel

1 red sugar-coated jube
(gummy candy)

1 red jelly snake
(gummy snake)

2 orange jelly snakes
(gummy snakes)

2 flying-saucer-shaped
sherberts

1 Use a sharp knife to level the tops of the cakes, if necessary. Place the cakes side by side on a work surface. Join the cakes at the long sides with a little buttercream. Position the template on the cakes and secure with toothpicks. Cut out around the sunshine face shape using a small sharp knife. Place the cake on the cake board.

2 Tint the buttercream with the yellow food colouring to the desired colour. Tint ½ cup of the yellow buttercream with the orange food colouring to the desired colour. Spread the yellow buttercream all over the cake. Wipe strokes of orange buttercream over the sunbursts to give highlights.

3 For the eyes, stick one red jellybean on each marshmallow using a little buttercream. For the pupils, pipe a small line on each jelly bean using the black writing gel.

4 Cut the heads from the red and orange snakes. Using the picture as a guide, position the eyes then the flying saucers for the cheeks and the snakes for the eyebrows and mouth on the cake.

You will need a 40 cm (16 inch)
square cake board for this cake.

Use candy-coated chocolate chips
to create a shadow around the
bottom edge of the cake.

★ Creepy Crawly Caterpillar

Decorating Time: 1 hour

17 × 80 ml (2½ fl oz/⅓ cup)
vanilla cupcakes in red
paper cases (recipe page
142, see tip)
185 ml (6 fl oz/¾ cup) large
vanilla cupcake (see tip)
2 quantities vanilla
buttercream (recipe
page 145)
Orange and green food
colourings

50 g (1¾ oz/¼ cup) sugar
7 spearmint leaf-shaped
sugar-coated jubes (gummy
candies), halved lengthways
1 red round sugar-coated
jube (gummy candy)
20 cm (8 inch) black licorice
strap

1 Use a sharp knife to level the tops
of the cakes, if necessary. Tint ⅓ cup
of the buttercream with the orange
food colouring to the desired colour.
Divide the remaining buttercream
into two bowls. Tint one bowl of
buttercream dark green and the
remaining bowl light green. Place
the sugar into a snaplock bag.
Add a few drops of the green food
colouring. Seal the bag and rub the
sugar through the bag until the sugar
is tinted green.

2 For the body, use a piping (icing) bag fitted with a large star tip to pipe dark green buttercream over half the small cupcakes. Use a clean piping bag with a large star tip to pipe light green buttercream over the remaining small cupcakes.

3 For the head, spread orange buttercream all over the large cupcake. Position the orange cupcake on the board. Arrange the green cupcakes, alternately, for the body. Sprinkle green sugar over half the green cupcakes. Arrange the spearmint leaves on the remaining green cupcakes.

4 For the face and using the picture as a guide, place the red jube halves on the orange cupcake for the eyes. Cut a strip of licorice for the mouth. Cut two 3 cm (1¼ inch) lengths of licorice for the antennae and 16 × 2 cm (¾ inch) lengths for the legs. Using the picture as a guide, position the antennae and legs on the cake.

TIP: For this recipe you will need 1½ quantities of vanilla buttercake. Spoon ½ cup of the mixture into one greased 185 ml (6 fl oz/¾ cup) large cupcake/muffin tin hole and bake for 20–25 minutes. Spoon the remaining cake mixture into 80 ml (2½ fl oz/⅓ cup) cupcake/muffin tin holes and bake for 20 minutes.

You will need a 40 x 50 cm (16 x 20 inch) rectangular cake board for this cake.

★ Lickable Lollipop

Decorating Time: 1 hour

24 cm (9½ inch) round
vanilla buttercake (recipe
page 142)

1½ quantities vanilla
buttercream (recipe
page 145)

Orange food colouring

12 jelly pythons (large
gummy snakes)

1.5 m (60 inch) × 1 cm
(½ inch) wide red
velvet ribbon

30 × 1 cm diameter
(12 × ½ inch) wooden stick

1 Use a sharp knife to level the top of the cake, if necessary. Tint the buttercream with the orange food colouring to the desired colour. Position the cake on the board. Spread the orange buttercream over the top and sides of the cake.

2 For the lollipop stick, wrap 1 metre (40 inch) of the ribbon around the stick. Tie the remaining ribbon in a bow around the top of the stick. Position the stick in the bottom of the cake.

3 Trim the heads from the pythons and discard. Starting in the centre of the cake, tightly coil the pythons to cover the entire cake surface, creating a lollipop effect.

You will need a 30 cm
(12 inch) round cake
board for this cake.

★ Tea party

Decorating Time: 1 hour

- 20 cm (8 inch) round vanilla buttercake (recipe page 142)
- ½ quantity vanilla buttercream (recipe page 145)
- 500 g (1 lb 2 oz) white fondant icing
- Pink food colouring
- Icing (confectioner's) sugar, sifted
- Miniature plastic tea set

1 Use a sharp knife to level the top of the cake, if necessary. Turn the cake upside down so the base becomes the top. Spread the cake all over with the buttercream.

2 For the flowers, tint 100 g (3½ oz) of the white fondant icing with the pink food colouring to the desired colour. Knead the pink fondant on a work surface lightly dusted with the sifted icing sugar until smooth. Roll on the work surface to 5 mm (¼ inch) thick. Using a 3 cm (1¼ inch) flower cutter, cut out small flowers.

3 For the tablecloth, tint the remaining white fondant with the pink food colouring to the desired colour. Knead on a work surface lightly dusted with the sifted icing sugar until smooth. Roll on the work surface to 6 mm (¼ inch) thick, forming a 28 cm (11¼ inch) circle, large enough to cover the cake and drape over the sides.

4 Using a rolling pin, gently lift the fondant onto the cake, allowing it to fall gently down and drape around the cake like a tablecloth. Use your hand to smooth the top.

5 Attach the pink flowers to the cake using a little water. Decorate with the tea set.

You will need a 25 cm (10 inch) round cake board for this cake.

Use green coloured coconut for grass on the board.

The Basics

Getting Started

Even though the decoration of your cake is important, it must taste delicious. It's the combination of the baking and decorating that will make your cake a star.

This chapter will tell you all you need to know about baking different kinds of cakes, covering them with buttercream and fondant icing, placing them on boards and creating the designs.

Here you will also find the basic cake recipes and the different icings or frostings that are used in the recipes. Different techniques to make the job easier are also included.

Timing is the most important part of cake decorating. You need to allow enough time for baking and cooling before decorating can begin. You can also save time by using packet cake mixes or even buying ready-made cakes. The thing to remember is that it should be fun from beginning to end.

KITCHEN ESSENTIALS

At the beginning of each recipe you will find a list of ingredients to decorate the cake photographed.

As well as these, you will need some tools that most kitchens will have. An electric mixer is essential to prepare the cake batter as well as cake tins in the size and shape required for the recipe. If several cake tins are needed, these can be borrowed from friends and family. This book includes templates for the more complex shapes but special-shaped cake tins can be hired from cake decorating shops.

You may also need a sharp knife, scissors, a rolling pin, a palette knife for spreading buttercream, cutters of different shapes to cut out fondant icing, and a small paintbrush, depending on the recipe you choose.

Also listed are food colourings. Liquid colours are available in any supermarket. Paste colourings give

more intense colour than liquids, particularly with bright hues, and are available from speciality kitchenware stores and cake decorating suppliers. Remember the colours can be changed to suit the party or the child.

The templates supplied are best traced using non-stick baking paper (parchment) which you will also need to line the cake tins. You'll also need some plastic wrap to keep the icings fresh.

BAKING THE CAKE

Each of the recipe designs in this book state the time it will take to decorate the cake. On top of this you must allow baking time for the actual cake bases. Depending on your oven size and the number of cake tins you own, you might have to bake the cakes in stages. Also remember that the cakes must be completely cooled before you begin decorating.

So put aside a few hours before you plan to decorate to enable you to make the cakes. It's probably best to do all the baking the day before you plan to decorate.

WHICH CAKE TO MAKE

Each of the cake designs tells you exactly the kind of cake you need to bake and what shape and size cake tin to bake it in. Follow the basic recipes on pages 142–144 and refer to the table on page 146 to guide you with quantities and cooking times.

SERVING QUANTITIES

The number of serves is not stated in the cake recipes because these are kids' cakes and usually one cake does any number of kids. Unless you are having a very large gathering that includes a number of adults, one of these cake designs should easily handle any kids' party.

ADAPTING THE RECIPES

Cake decorating is a fun art that allows you to express your individuality or that of the child. So remember, the cake colours and even shapes can be altered as you wish. Covering the cake with buttercream is the easiest as it can be smoothed out if you aren't happy with your decoration allowing you to begin again. If you are a beginner to cake decorating, stick with one of the designs in the book first and it will give you the confidence to make changes next time.

★ Vanilla Buttercake

Preparation time: 15 minutes
Cooking time: 50 minutes
Makes: 20 cm (8 inch) round cake/1 quantity (for other sizes and shapes
  see table page 146)

185 g (6½ oz/1¼ cups)
  self-raising flour
50 g (1¾ oz/⅓ cup) plain
  (all-purpose) flour
165 g (5¾ oz/¾ cup)
  caster (superfine) sugar
125 g (4½ oz) unsalted
  butter, softened
3 eggs, at room
  temperature
60 ml (2 fl oz/¼ cup) milk
1 teaspoon vanilla extract

1 Preheat oven to 180°C (350°F/Gas 4). Grease a 20 cm (8 inch) round cake tin and line the base and side with baking paper (parchment), (see page 150).

2 Sift the flours into a mixing bowl. Add the sugar, butter, eggs, milk and vanilla. Using an electric mixer, beat on low speed until combined. Increase the speed to medium and beat for 2–3 minutes or until well combined and the mixture is pale in colour.

3 Spoon the mixture into the prepared tin and smooth the surface with the back of a spoon. Bake in the centre of the oven for 45–50 minutes or until a skewer inserted into the centre of the cake comes out clean. Cool the cake in the tin for 5 minutes before turning out onto a wire rack. Allow to cool completely.

TIPS: If you require a half quantity of buttercake, halve all of the ingredients except for the eggs and milk. Use 2 eggs and 1 tablespoon milk.

This cake will keep in an airtight container for up to 3 days. It can be frozen, without decoration, for up to 2 months. Wrap tightly in plastic wrap and then place in a freezer bag and seal. It's a good idea to write the date on the bag.

VARIATIONS
Any of these flavour variations can be used depending on your child's preference.

Chocolate Buttercake: Replace 30 g (1 oz) of the plain (all-purpose) flour with 30 g (1 oz) unsweetened cocoa powder and sift with the flour.
Orange Buttercake: Replace the vanilla extract with the finely grated zest of 1 orange.
Lemon Buttercake: Replace the vanilla extract with the finely grated zest of 2 lemons.

★ Gluten-Free Buttercake

Preparation time: 15 minutes
Cooking time: 40 minutes
Makes: 20 cm (8 inch) round cake/1 quantity (for other sizes and shapes
see table page 146; note that cooking times for this gluten-free buttercake
will be 5–15 minutes less than those specified)

200 g (7 oz/1⅓ cups)
gluten-free self-raising
flour
165 g (5¾ oz/¾ cup)
caster (superfine) sugar
150 g (5½ oz) unsalted
butter, softened
60 ml (2 fl oz/¼ cup) milk
3 eggs, at room
temperature
1 teaspoon vanilla extract

1 Preheat oven to 180°C (350°F/Gas 4). Grease a 20 cm (8 inch) round cake tin and line the base and side with baking paper (parchment), (see page 150).

2 Sift the flour and 60 g (2¼ oz/¼ cup) of the sugar into a bowl. Using an electric mixer, beat the butter in a small bowl for 4–5 minutes or until pale and creamy. Gradually beat in the flour and sugar mixture and the milk until just combined. Transfer to a large bowl.

3 Using an electric mixer with a whisk attachment, whisk the eggs, vanilla and remaining sugar in a medium bowl for about 5–6 minutes or until very thick and pale and tripled in volume. Using a spatula or large metal spoon, stir half the egg mixture into the flour mixture. Fold in the remaining egg mixture until just combined.

3 Spoon the mixture into the prepared tin and smooth the surface with the back of a spoon. Bake in the centre of the oven for 35–40 minutes or until a skewer inserted into the centre of the cake comes out clean. Cool the cake in the tin for 5 minutes before turning out onto a rack to cool completely.

TIPS: If you require a half quantity of gluten-free buttercake, halve all of the ingredients except for the eggs and milk. Use 2 eggs and 1 tablespoon milk.

This cake will keep in an airtight container for up to 3 days. It can be frozen, without decoration, for up to 2 months. Wrap tightly in plastic wrap and then place in a freezer bag and seal. It's a good idea to write the date on the bag.

★ Chocolate Mud Cake

Preparation time: 20 minutes + 15 minutes cooling time
Cooking time: 1 hour 45 minutes
Makes: 24 cm (9½ inch) round cake/1 quantity (for other sizes and shapes
  see table page 147)

250 g (9 oz) unsalted
  butter
250 g (9 oz) dark (semi-
  sweet) chocolate, chopped
495 g (1 lb 2 oz/2¼ cups)
  caster (superfine) sugar
4 eggs, lightly whisked
125 ml (4 fl oz/½ cup) milk
150 g (5½ oz/1 cup)
  self-raising flour
150 g (5½ oz/1 cup) plain
  (all-purpose) flour
55 g (2 oz/½ cup)
  unsweetened cocoa
  powder, sifted

1   Preheat the oven to 160°C (315°F/ Gas 2–3). Lightly grease a deep 24 cm (9½ inch) round cake tin and line the base and side with baking paper (parchment), extending at least 5 cm (2 inch) above the top (see page 150).

2   Combine the butter, chocolate and sugar in a large saucepan with 185 ml (6 fl oz/¾ cup) hot water and stir over low heat until smooth. Remove from the heat. Transfer to a large bowl and cool for 15 minutes.

3   Whisk the eggs and milk into the chocolate mixture. Sift together the flours and the cocoa, then whisk into the chocolate and egg mixture to make a smooth batter.

4   Pour the mixture into the prepared tin and smooth the surface with the back of a spoon. Bake in the centre of the oven for 1¾ hours. Test the centre with a skewer. It should be slightly wet with crumbs but not coated in batter. Remove the cake from the oven. If the top looks raw, bake for another 5–10 minutes, then remove. Leave in the tin until completely cooled, then turn out.

TIP: Keep this cake in an airtight container in the refrigerator for up to 3 weeks or store in a cool, dry place for up to 1 week.

This cake can be frozen, without decoration, for up to 2 months. Wrap tightly in plastic wrap and then place in a freezer bag and seal. It's a good idea to write the date on the bag.

★ Vanilla Buttercream

Preparation time: 10 minutes
Makes: 1⅓ cups

125 g (4½ oz) unsalted
  butter, at room
  temperature (see tip)
215 g (7½ oz/1¾ cups)
  icing (confectioner's)
  sugar, sifted
1 tablespoon milk
1 teaspoon vanilla extract

1 Using an electric mixer, beat the butter in a medium bowl for 4–5 minutes or until it turns very pale. Gradually beat in the icing sugar until smooth and creamy, scraping down the sides of the bowl as necessary.

2 Add the milk and vanilla extract and beat until well combined. Use as desired.

TIPS: This buttercream is best used immediately. The consistency should be smooth and thick enough to hold its shape when piped. You can test by running your finger over the buttercream—it should hold its shape well but not be stiff. To adjust the consistency, if necessary, beat in a little more milk or icing sugar as needed. The more times you make and use buttercream the easier it will be to get the perfect consistency.

Buttercream will separate or curdle if the butter is too soft or you add too much liquid—milk or colouring. Make sure the butter is at room temperature and add the liquid very sparingly until the mixture is thick and spreadable. If your buttercream has curdled, it's best to begin again and make another batch.

VARIATIONS
Any of these flavour variations can be used depending on your child's preference.

Chocolate Buttercream: Reduce the icing sugar to 185 g (6½ oz/1½ cups). Sift 30 g (1 oz) unsweetened cocoa powder with the icing sugar before adding to the mixture in the second stage of beating.
Orange Buttercream: Replace the vanilla extract with the finely grated zest of 1 orange.
Lemon Buttercream: Replace the vanilla extract with the finely grated zest of 2 lemons.
Caramel Buttercream: Reduce the icing sugar to 215 g (7½ oz/1¾ cups). Omit the milk. Add 110 g (3¾ oz/½ cup) firmly packed brown sugar and 115 g (4 oz/⅓ cup) golden syrup (light corn syrup) with the vanilla for the first stage of beating. Then add the icing sugar in the second stage of beating.

★ Cake Cooking Guide

Vanilla/Gluten-Free Buttercake (Recipes pages 142–143) Oven: 180°C/350°F/Gas 4

Cake Tin Size (base measurement)	Quantity Vanilla or Gluten-Free Buttercake Recipe	Baking Time (less 5–15 minutes for Gluten-Free Buttercake)
20 cm (8 inch) round	1 quantity	45–50 minutes
22 cm (8½ inch) round	1½ quantities	1 hour
24 cm (9½ inch) round	2 quantities	1 hour 10 minutes
30 cm (12 inch) round	3 quantities	1 hour 20 minutes
18 × 23 cm (7 × 9 inch) oval	2 quantities	50–55 minutes
20 cm (8 inch) ring	1 quantity	40 minutes
20 cm (8 inch) square	1 quantity	50–60 minutes
23 cm (9 inch) square	2 quantities	1 hour 10 minutes
25 cm (10 inch) square	3 quantities	1 hour 20 minutes
30 cm (12 inch) square	4 quantities	1 hour 30 minutes
20 × 30 cm (8 × 12 inch) lamington/brownie/baking tin	1 quantity	30 minutes
26 × 35 cm (10½ × 14 inch) baking dish	2 quantities	50–55 minutes
9 × 19 cm (3½ × 7½ inch) loaf bar tin	1 quantity	50–55 minutes
8 × 20 cm (3¼ × 8 inch) nut roll tin	½ quantity	1 hour 10 minutes
1 litre (35 fl oz/4 cup) pudding basin	1 quantity	1 hour
2.5 litre (10 cup) dolly varden cake tin	2½ quantities	1 hour 15 minutes
12-hole 20 ml (½ fl oz) mini cupcake/muffin tin	½ quantity	10 minutes
12-hole 40 ml (1¼ fl oz) patty cake tin	½ quantity	15 minutes
12-hole 80 ml (2½ fl oz/⅓ cup) cupcake/muffin tin	1 quantity	20–25 minutes
12-hole 185 ml (6 fl oz/¾ cup) large (texas) cupcake/muffin tin	2 quantities	30 minutes

Chocolate Mud Cake (Recipe page 144) Oven: 160°C/315°F/Gas 2–3

Cake Tin Size (base measurement)	Quantity of Chocolate Mud Cake Recipe	Baking Time
24 cm (9½ inch) round	1 quantity	1 hour 45 minutes
30 cm (12 inch) round	2½ quantities	2 hours 20 minutes
25 cm (10 inch) square	2 quantities	2 hours
30 cm (12 inch) square	2½ quantities	2 hours 15 minutes
20 × 30 cm (8 × 12 inch) lamington/brownie/baking tin	½ quantity	35–40 minutes
26 × 35 cm (10½ × 14 inch) baking dish	2 quantities	2 hours

★ Meringue Frosting

Preparation time: 15 minutes
Cooking time: 5 minutes
Makes: 2½ cups

165 g (5¾ oz/¾ cup) caster (superfine) sugar
3 egg whites, at room temperature
300 g (10½ oz) unsalted butter, cubed, at room temperature
1½ teaspoons vanilla extract

1   Half-fill a medium saucepan with water. Bring to a simmer over medium heat.

2   Combine the sugar and egg whites in a heatproof bowl large enough to sit snugly into the saucepan without touching the water. Reduce the heat to medium–low. Place the bowl over the simmering water and whisk for 4–5 minutes or until the sugar dissolves and the mixture is hot.

3   Transfer the mixture to the bowl of an electric mixer with a whisk attachment and whisk on medium–high speed for about 8 minutes or until thick and glossy and the mixture has cooled to room temperature.

4   Reduce the speed to medium then whisk in the butter, a little at a time, until the butter is incorporated and the mixture is smooth. Whisk in the vanilla.

5   Beat the frosting with a wooden spoon or a beater attachment for 1–2 minutes to expel any air pockets. Use immediately.

★ Vanilla Glace Icing

Preparation time: 5 minutes
Makes: 1 cup

405 g (14¼ oz/3¼ cups) icing (confectioner's) sugar, sifted (see tip)
60 ml (2 fl oz/¼ cup) water, at room temperature
1 teaspoon vanilla extract

1   Place the icing sugar in a medium bowl. Use a spatula or wooden spoon to slowly stir in the water until the mixture is smooth and has a heavy coating consistency. (You may not need all the water.) Stir in the vanilla. Add a little more water, if desired, to reach a lighter spreading consistency.

TIP: Use pure icing sugar. Icing sugar mixture is not suitable for this recipe.

★ Dark Chocolate Ganache

Preparation time: 5 minutes + 30–60 minutes chilling
Cooking time: 5 minutes
Makes: 1¼ cups

250 g (9 oz) good-quality dark (bittersweet) chocolate, chopped
185 ml (6 fl oz/¾ cups) pouring cream

1 Place the chocolate in a medium heatproof bowl and set aside. Heat the cream in a small saucepan over medium heat until simmering. Pour the cream over the chocolate and set aside for 2–3 minutes. Stir until the chocolate melts and the mixture is well combined.

2 Refrigerate for 30–60 minutes, stirring often, or until the mixture is a thick spreadable consistency.

VARIATIONS

Any of these flavour variations can be used depending on your child's preference.

Milk Chocolate Ganache: Replace the dark chocolate with milk chocolate.
White Chocolate Ganache: Replace the dark chocolate with white chocolate.
Whipped Chocolate Ganache: Chill the dark, milk or white chocolate ganache for at least 45–60 minutes or until thick but not firm. Use electric beaters to beat the ganache for 1–2 minutes or until thickened and slightly paler in colour. Makes 1½ cups.

Lining Cake Tins

Cake tins are lined to prevent cakes sticking to them during baking. The following methods of lining are suitable for most simple shapes. Before lining with non-stick baking paper (parchment), lightly grease the cake tin with melted unsalted butter or a mild-flavoured vegetable oil spray. This helps to keep the lining paper in place.

TO LINE A ROUND OR OVAL TIN

Cut a strip of paper long enough to go around the outside of the tin and 2.5 cm (1 inch) taller than the height of the tin. Fold down a cuff about 2 cm (¾ inch) deep along the length of the strip. Cut the folded cuff diagonally at 1 cm (½ inch) intervals. Fit the paper strip around the inside of the tin, with the cuts on the base of the tin, pressing the cuts out at right angles so they sit flat on the base. Place the cake tin on another sheet of paper and draw around it. Cut out the circle and place it in the base of the tin.

TO LINE A SQUARE OR RECTANGULAR TIN

Use the same method as for a round tin (left) or if you are in a hurry, place the tin on a double sheet of paper and draw around it to make a square the same size as the base of the tin. Place this in the tin and press it onto the base. Cut a strip of paper long enough to fit around the edge of the tin and 2.5 cm (1 inch) taller than the height of the tin. Place this around the inside edge of the tin, fitting it into the corners.

TO LINE AN UNUSUAL-SHAPED TIN

Follow the instructions for lining the side of a round tin (left). Draw around the outside of the tin, as before, to make a lining for the base and place this on top of the cuts.

Using Buttercream

Buttercream is a spreadable, easy-to-use icing that can be smoothed or roughed up to give texture as required. It is easily coloured and piped or used between layers. It is often used under fondant icing to seal the cake crumbs and also give the cake a delicious taste.

COVERING A CAKE WITH BUTTERCREAM

For the top, place a large spoonful of buttercream in the centre of the top and, using a palette knife, spread the buttercream across the top just like spreading butter. Smooth the buttercream over the surface of the cake, keeping the knife quite flat to eliminate any air bubbles. Continue until the top of the cake is completely covered.

For the side, using the same 'buttering' action, apply the buttercream holding the palette knife vertically and positioning your finger down the back of the blade to apply pressure to the icing and disperse any air bubbles.

To smooth the surface, wash the palette knife completely. Fill a glass with hot water and dip the palette knife in the glass to warm the blade. Remove, dry and use to smooth over the buttercream. Continue to clean, dip and dry the palette knife as required until the buttercream is as smooth as possible.

Piping Decorations

PIPING BAGS

You can buy piping (icing) bags made of plastic, nylon or jaconette or you can use a piping syringe. They are all available from kitchenware stores and cake decorating suppliers. Disposable bags are available from the supermarket. You can also make your own bags with paper. To do this, cut a 25 cm (10 inch) square of non-stick baking paper (parchment) in half diagonally to make two triangles. Twist both triangles to make two cones and secure with tape. Cut off 1 cm (½ inch) of the tip and fit a piping tube inside the bag. Make all the bags needed before you start: if you are using different coloured icings, you will need a different bag for each.

TIPS, TUBES AND NOZZLES

These are available in almost any shape or size. Shapes vary from plain round to stars, curves, flat and crosses. The sizes are universal measures with number 000 being the finest. Simple shapes are available from the supermarket but the best place for supplies is a speciality kitchenware store or cake decorating supplier.

Generally, the smaller the tip or tube, the thinner the icing consistency should be. Also, the smaller the tip you are using, the finer the work and the smaller the bag should be, to give you maximum control.

PIPING TECHNIQUES

Fill the piping bag only two-thirds full—if you put too much in, icing may seep from the top—and then twist or fold over the top of the bag. It is best to hold the piping bag with two hands for better control, however experienced you are.

For paper piping bags, use the index finger of one hand to support the bag underneath, with the thumb keeping the bag closed at the top and to apply pressure to the bag.

Alternatively, if you are using a nylon or jaconette bag, nestle the bag between your thumb and index finger, using the remaining fingers to apply pressure to the bag.

Rest the index finger of the other hand against the base of the bag to guide the tube and prevent your hand shaking through the application of pressure. Apply pressure from the top of the bag forcing the icing down to the tip.

Line—Use a plain round tip. Hold the bag at a 60 degree angle, just touching the tip on the surface, squeeze with even pressure and slowly pull away. (see Fairy Princess Castle, page 87).

Lines can also be added using writing gel which is available in tubes from the supermarket. These small tubes are easy to control and are the best for writing on cakes.

Zigzag or Squiggle—Use a plain round tip for plain zigzags. Or use a star tip if you wish the lines to be very squiggly. Pipe short lines, releasing the pressure and lifting off at the end of each line (see Rainbow Butterfly, page 74).

Star—Use a small or large star tip. Hold the bag upright, squeeze out the icing and then pull up into a point. These can be piped in a border or used to cover a large area on the top or side of a cake (see Creepy Crawly Caterpillar, page 130).

Rosette—Tips for rosettes are similar to star tips but have finer indentations. Hold the bag almost upright and squeeze, moving the bag in a circular motion and lifting slightly. To finish, bring the tip to the centre, relax the pressure and pull off (see left).

Shell Border—Shells can be piped using a plain or star tip. Hold the bag at a 45 degree angle and squeeze to make a bulb. Reducing the pressure, sweep the tube down towards the surface to form the tail. Make the next shell over the tail of the previous shell to form a border (see The Giant Slice, page 105).

Using Fondant Icing

Fondant icing is a good starting place for anyone new to cake decorating. It is relatively easy and effective to use if a few things are kept in mind. It can be sticky in humid weather and although water is used to stick pieces together, it will leave marks on the fondant surface. So keep water well away during rolling.

Fondant is soft and pliable, easily coloured and shaped, and very exciting to work with ... and if things do go wrong, you can simply roll it out again.

Fondant icing is also known as soft icing, rolled fondant or RTR (ready to roll) and is available from supermarkets, speciality kitchenware stores, cake decorating suppliers and online. It can also be purchased already coloured. Keep fondant icing wrapped well in plastic wrap until you are ready to use it, to prevent it drying out. Unused fondant icing can be rewrapped and sealed and stored in the fridge for several weeks.

TINTING OR COLOURING FONDANT ICING

Fondant icing can be coloured any shade of the colour spectrum, and mixing and experimenting with colours can be very rewarding. You can buy ready-coloured fondant icing or colour your own while it is still soft.

The easiest way to colour fondant is by adding paste or liquid food colouring (paste is usually better quality, will give a stronger colour and is easier to use with fondant). When using any colourings, never pour them directly from the bottle—use a dropper or toothpick and add sparingly.

To tint or colour fondant, knead lightly on a work surface lightly dusted with icing (confectioner's) sugar, then dip the end of a toothpick into the food colouring and wipe it onto the fondant (remember that a little colour can go a long way, so add a little at a time, especially if you want soft colours). Knead again until the colour is very evenly distributed—check by cutting the fondant in half, and then continue kneading if necessary.

Once you've reached the right colour, wrap the fondant icing in plastic and seal in a snaplock bag or airtight container until you're ready to use it.

Kids' Party Cakes

MARBLING FONDANT ICING

Marbling is achieved by partially blending two different colours of fondant icing to create streaks. Twist two coloured strips of fondant together, and then knead gently until a marble effect is achieved (see The Giant Slice, page 104).

Alternatively, knead white fondant until pliable and add random drops of paste or liquid colouring before folding and twisting the fondant until the colour starts to streak.

The more you knead the icing, the less obvious the marbling will be, so don't overwork it.

STENCILLING FONDANT ICING

Stencilling is done on fondant that is already rolled and usually on a cake that is already covered in fondant.

You can use your own template or a stencil to add a specific design on fondant once it is dry. Stencils are readily available at craft stores and online. Choose a stencil that suits your cake theme.

Hold the stencil gently but evenly against the fondant. Place a little liquid colour or colour paste diluted with a little water in a small dish. Dip a small piece of sponge in the desired colour—don't saturate it with liquid, it needs to be just damp.

Practise on a spare piece of fondant first to get the right effect and intensity of colour, then work directly on the cake.

If you like, mask off any areas of the cake that you don't want to colour by using a piece of baking paper (parchment). Sponge the cake with the colour, then gently lift off the masking paper and let the pattern dry (see Gift Box, page 112).

You can use more than one colour but it's best to mask off the different coloured areas of the stencil or template. To avoid smudging, wait until one colour is completely dry before applying the next.

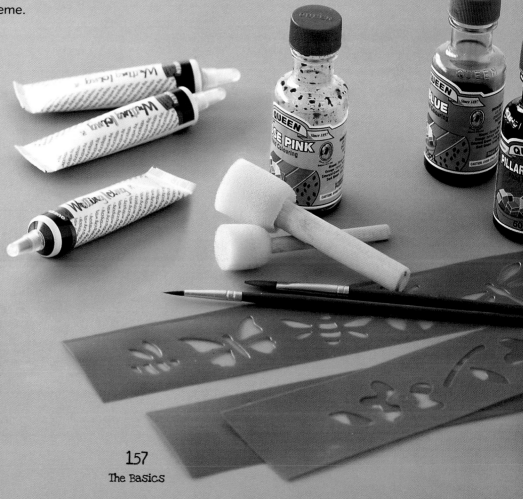

Using Fondant Icing (continued)

HAND PAINTING FONDANT ICING

Painting is good for adding details such as eyes and mouths to characters, or free-painting scenes onto plain iced cakes or plaques to be attached to cakes. Use food colourings, piping gels or piping icings. Before applying any colour, ensure the fondant is completely dry and firm to the touch. Use a very fine brush and don't overload the brush or the fondant will be too wet and make the colour streaky. Dip your brush lightly in the colour then dab off any excess on a sheet of kitchen paper before painting.

ROLLING OUT FONDANT ICING

Knead the fondant icing on a work surface lightly dusted with icing (confectioner's) sugar until pliable. If you are going to colour the fondant icing, do it at this stage (see page 156). Roll out the fondant icing to the thickness and size required for the recipe. Move the fondant icing often on the work surface to prevent sticking.

COVERING A CAKE WITH FONDANT ICING

This method is suitable for covering both round cakes and cakes with corners. Once you have rolled out your fondant icing work quickly so it doesn't dry out and crack. To give more control and prevent tearing the fondant icing as you lift it, roll it over the rolling pin, then carefully lift it and move it across onto the cake, unrolling and smoothing it over the top and side. Dust your hands lightly with icing (confectioner's) sugar and rub them firmly down and over the cake to smooth the fondant and remove any folds or wrinkles. If a fold or crease occurs in the icing, carefully lift it out from the side of the cake and gently ease it on again, smoothing as you go.

Once the icing is smooth, trim off any excess from around the base with a sharp knife. Wrap the trimmings and any leftover fondant well in plastic wrap and seal in a snaplock bag or airtight container and store in a cool dry place. They may be needed to complete your design or they can be used on another cake.

Any air bubbles in the fondant can be pierced with a pin. Then use your hand to smooth the fondant and remove the mark.

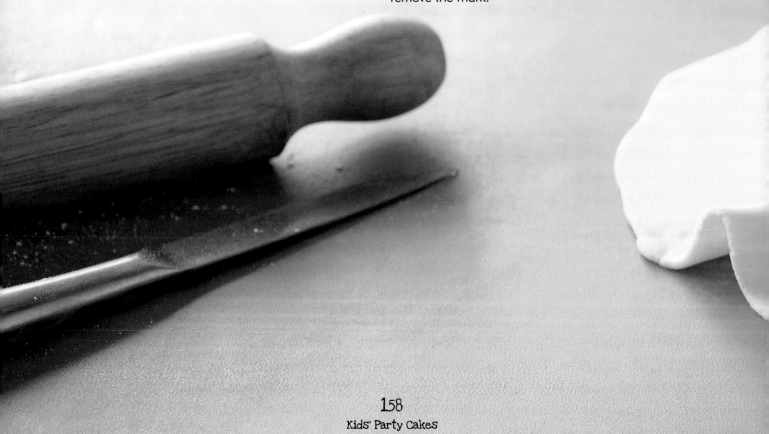

Smooth over the fondant again with the palm of your hands or an icing smoother (wide plastic scraper), keeping your hands lightly dusted with icing sugar to prevent them sticking.

TIP: If you wish to cover the cake before positioning on the board, place a sheet of non-stick baking paper (parchment) under the cake before covering or decorating. Allow the edges of the paper to stick out around the cake. This will act as a sling to help move the cake to the final board. This makes it easier to transfer the cake to the board without putting fingerprints in the icing and also protects the cake from contact with the board—sometimes the colour from the board can stain the edge of the fondant. Secure the paper under the cake to the board and then trim away the paper from around the cake with a scalpel or tiny scissors so that it can't be seen.

PLACING A CAKE ON THE BOARD

Once the fondant is completely dry, spread a little buttercream or moistened fondant icing onto your cake board (this will help secure the cake to the board). Then transfer the cake to the board with two egg flips or by using the baking paper (parchment) underneath as a sling (see tip).

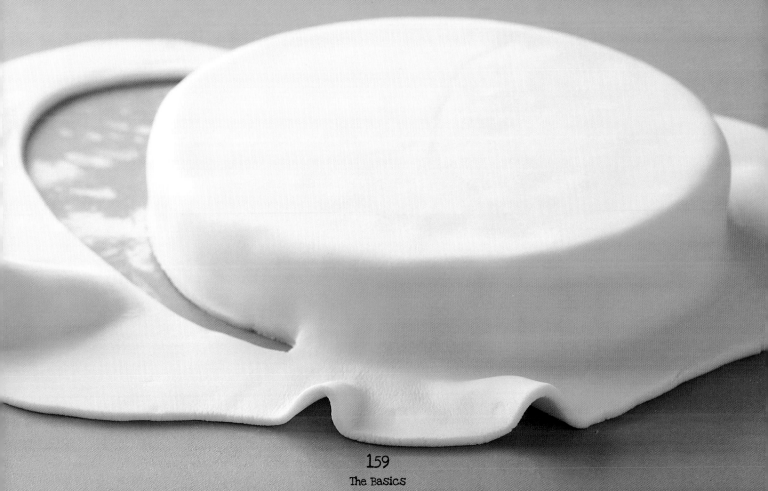

159
The Basics

Cake Boards

Cake boards are used to support and transport cakes. You can buy boards or cut them to size from heavy-duty cardboard (for light cakes) or thin sheets of chipboard or MDF that can be cut to size at a hardware store. Purchased cake boards are usually already covered in foil and are available from speciality kitchenware stores and cake decorating suppliers.

You can cover your own boards with coloured paper, fabric, coloured adhesive plastic or even fondant icing.

Some porous papers and all fabrics will absorb oils from the cake and stain. If you're worried about this, cover the paper or fabric with clear adhesive plastic or place a layer of non-stick baking paper (parchment) between the cake and the board.

Cake boards can be cleaned and stored for future use.

COVERING BOARDS WITH PAPER OR FABRIC

To cover a cake board, place the board face down on the back of the sheet of paper or fabric. Trace around the board then draw an outline 5 cm (2 inch) outside this line and cut out the larger outline. Make diagonal cuts 1 cm (½ inch) apart around the edge, cutting in as far as the smaller outline. Brush the board face with non-toxic glue and press firmly onto the back of the paper or fabric. Press or roll out any air bubbles. Fold the cut edges over and secure with tape or glue. Cut another sheet of paper slightly smaller than the board and glue over the base of the board to hide the cut edges. You can also cover the edges with a ribbon the same width as the thickness of the board to give the edge a neat finish.

Remember that paper can tear easily, especially if you're using glue, which will soften the paper.

Edible ★ Decorations

1 Shell chocolates
2 Ice-cream cones
3 Sour and fruit straps
4 Musk ring-shaped hard candies
5 Candy-coated chocolate chips
6 Chocolate-coated licorice bullets
7 Candy sticks
8 Fruit-flavoured cereal rings
9 White chocolate chips
10 Milk chocolate melts
11 Multi-coloured jelly snakes (gummy snakes)
12 Licorice pieces and licorice twists
13 Mini candy-coated chocolate buttons
14 Animal-shaped soft candies
15 Jelly beans
16 White rectangular mini hard candies
17 Coloured sprinkles
18 Spearmint leaf-shaped sugar-coated jubes
19 Mini marshmallows
20 Teardrop and round marshmallows
21 Mini jubes (gumdrops)

22 Fairy floss
23 Jelly snakes
24 Triangular chocolate and nougat bar
25 Candy-coated chocolate buttons
26 Gold wrapped chocolate money
27 Banana-shaped soft yellow candies
28 Lollipops
29 Chocolate mint sticks
30 Silver cachous
31 Ice-cream shaped soft candies
32 White chocolate melts
33 Candy-coated chocolate buttons
34 Round coloured candies
35 Red licorice twists
36 Chocolate-coated finger biscuits
37 Chocolate-coated mint biscuits
38 Chocolate-coated wafers
39 Ice-cream wafers
40 Black licorice strap
41 Sugar-coated jubes
42 Flying saucer-shaped sherberts
43 Milk bottle-shaped soft candies
44 Mini rock candies
45 White chocolate bars
46 Sprinkle-coated chocolate buttons
47 Candy-coated fruit buttons
48 Chocolate-coated caramel lattice
49 Ring-shaped hard candies

Index

Published in 2012 by Murdoch Books Pty Limited

Murdoch Books Australia
Pier 8/9
23 Hickson Road
Millers Point NSW 2000
Phone: +61 (0) 2 8220 2000
Fax: +61 (0) 2 8220 2558
www.murdochbooks.com.au
info@murdochbooks.com.au

Murdoch Books UK Limited
Erico House, 6th Floor
93–99 Upper Richmond Road
Putney, London SW15 2TG
Phone: +44 (0) 20 8785 5995
Fax: +44 (0) 20 8785 5985
www.murdochbooks.co.uk
info@murdochbooks.co.uk

For Corporate Orders & Custom Publishing contact Noel Hammond,
National Business Development Manager Murdoch Books Australia

Publisher: Anneka Manning
Project Manager: Laura Wilson
Copyeditor: Carol Jacobson
Food Editor: Cathie Lonnie
Designer: Tania Gomes
Photographer: Steve Brown
Stylist: Vanessa Austin
Production Controller: Joan Beal

Recipe development: Adam Cremona, Nicole Dicker, Kathy Knudsen and Kirrily La Rosa
Home Economists: Adam Cremona, Kim Meredith and Kirrily La Rosa

National Library of Australia Cataloguing-in-Publication Data

Title:	Kids' party cakes: 50 fun, fast and fabulous ideas
ISBN:	978-1-74266-541-2 (pbk.)
Notes:	Includes index.
Subjects:	Cake.
	Cake decorating.
	Children's parties.
Dewey Number:	641.8653

A catalogue record for this book is available from the British Library.

Printed by C & C Offset Printing Co. Ltd, China.

The Publisher and stylist would like to thank Paper Eskimo, Spotlight, Dulux, No chintz, Mud Australia, Specklefarm, Lark
and the Queen Bee Party Shop for lending equipment for use and photography.

IMPORTANT: Those who might be at risk from the effects of salmonella poisoning (the elderly, pregnant women, young children and those suffering from immune deficiency diseases) should consult their doctor with any concerns about eating raw eggs.

CONVERSION GUIDE: You may find cooking times vary depending on the oven you are using. For fan-forced ovens, as a general rule, set the oven temperature to 20°C (35°F) lower than indicated in the recipe. We have used 20 ml (4 teaspoon) tablespoon measures. If you are using a 15 ml (3 teaspoon) tablespoon, for most recipes the difference will not be noticeable. However, for recipes using baking powder, gelatine, bicarbonate of soda (baking soda), small amounts of flour and cornflour (cornstarch), add an extra teaspoon for each tablespoon specified.

On the cover: Yellow Kite (page 122–3)